Great Quotes from

Feisty Women

Dream Big... Be Feisty!

Great Quotes from

Feisty Women

Ava Diamond

FEISTY WOMAN:
One who is vibrant, gutsy, lives
boldly, is true to herself, and
embraces her power as a woman

Sage Creek Press
FORT COLLINS, COLORADO

Grateful acknowledgement is made to the following for permission to reprint copyrighted material:
For *Wisdom of the Heart* © 2002 by Alan Cohen
reprinted by permission from Alan Cohen.

ALAN COHEN is the author of many popular inspirational books, including the bestselling *The Dragon Doesn't Live Here Anymore*, the award-winning *A Deep Breath of Life* and
most recently *Mr. Everit's Secret: What I Learned From the World's Richest Man*. Alan offers *Living
Prosperously*, a home-study course in creating greater abundance, and the life-transforming
Mastery Training in Maui. For information call 800-568-3079, visit www.alancohen.com,
email info@alancohen.com, or write P.O. Box 835, Haiku, HI 96708

For *The Path to Love* © 1997 by Deepak Chopra, M.D.
reprinted by permission from the executive office
of Deepak Chopra

PUBLISHED BY Sage Creek Press
Post Office Box 8181
Fort Collins, CO 80526

Printed and bound in the United States of America

© 2005 by Ava Diamond
Illustrations © 2004 Ilan Shamir, pages 1, 3, 13, 43, 73, 101,
129, 160, and back cover; www.YourTrueNature.com

ISBN 0-9760968-0-3
Library of Congress Control Number: 2004095747

Book and cover design by Rebecca Finkel

Quantity discounts are available on bulk purchases of this book for
education, gift or premium purchases. Contact Sage Creek Press.

Visit our website at www.feistywomen.com

DEDICATION

To my mom, Lila Diamond,

who was the first

Feisty Woman in my life.

Through her example, I gained

the courage to be fully who I am.

And to all Feisty Women

who live with truth and passion.

6

ACKNOWLEDGMENTS

My heart is filled with gratitude for:

Jo Cunningham, for her encouragement, support and love through this project.

Brad Wilkinson, editor extraordinaire, who in the second decade of our friendship brings truth and fun to our work and our play.

Ilan Shamir, whose illustrations enliven these pages.

Leane Gabel, Matthew Quigley, and Nettie Grodecki for their feedback and suggestions on the manuscript. Thanks, Leane, for suggesting I include biographical information.

Rebecca Finkel, who designed the feisty-est book ever.

Allen Klein, whose expertise in writing quotations books provided me with direction at the beginning stages of this project.

Jean Anderson of the Fort Collins Public Library and Naomi Lederer of the Colorado State University Library for their expert research assistance.

Leslie Ann Gibson, who compiled and arranged *The Women's Book of Positive Quotations,* the source of many of these quotes.

Scott Horton, LeAnn Thieman, Tina Diamond, Michael Bell, and Melanie Miller for their support and encouragement through the process of writing this book.

C O N T E N T S

A PERSONAL NOTE FROM Ava Diamond

My intention in writing this book is to celebrate and affirm the wisdom and power of feisty women. As I pored over thousands of quotations, I was struck by the intelligence, clarity and understanding that women share with the world.

This book started out to be simply a collection of uplifting quotations. Yet the voices of these women spoke to my heart and moved me to share my own experience and insight with you.

For every woman who wants to live with joy, passion and gusto, this book is for you.

For every woman who has ever been told that she was *too much*, or needed to *tone it down*, this book is for you.

For every woman who wants to explore new territory, break through self-limiting beliefs, and experience new delights, this book is for you.

Savor these quotations. Marinate in them. Allow them to inspire and motivate you. Let these wise, feisty women speak to your soul. ⊚

Living with Joy and Fulfillment

We shall never know all the good that a simple smile can do.

MOTHER TERESA
1910–1997

Born Agnes Gonxha Bojaxhiu in Skopje, Yugoslavia (now Macedonia). Felt the call of God at age twelve, and knew she needed to be a missionary. Dedicated her life to helping the poor, the sick, and the dying. Spent much of her life in India. Started the Missionaries of Charity which ministers across the world. Received much acclaim and many awards, including the Nobel Prize for Peace in 1979.

Living with Joy and Fulfillment

Okay, let's face it. Most of us won't solve world hunger or single-handedly create world peace. And we don't have to.

What we *can* do is look around and see where we can make a difference. To live a fulfilling life, we can find ways to give of ourselves and to make the world a better place— one small action at a time.

I was flying home one night, and was in line at my favorite soul food restaurant in the Atlanta airport. The tall, middle aged woman behind the counter was heaping plates with fried chicken, fish, sweet potatoes and collard greens. For the moment, they were out of okra. The man in front of me began to yell at the woman behind the counter. "Why can't you keep things filled up? Don't you know people are in a hurry to catch their planes? What's the matter with you?" He was furious!

"I'm so sorry, sir...is there another vegetable I can get you? I'd be happy to give you some extra cornbread to make it up to you." The woman smiled at him and waited. "I'll just go get some pizza over there," he yelled as he stormed off.

She struggled to keep her composure, and was almost in tears. I was next. I took a moment to let my heart connect with hers. I looked her deeply in the eyes, smiled, and said, "It's okay, just breathe..." She took a moment to pull herself together, and then asked me for my order.

As she handed me my tray, she thanked me for being a blessing to her that night. "You don't know how much that meant," she whispered.

You never know how much your small kindness will mean to someone. Opportunities to have an impact are every-where—we just need to notice them and act on them.

Gratitude unlocks the fullness of life. It turns what we have into enough and more.

MELODY BEATTIE
Contemporary
Bestselling author known for her work on codependency. Books include
Codependent No More, *Beyond Codependency*, and *The Lessons of Love*.

When I was a little girl, my mom had a strict rule. When someone gave me a gift, I had to write them a thank-you note before I could play with or use the gift. I was also taught to say "thank you" whenever someone did something for me or gave me something.

Although I went through the motions as a child, it was a rote response. I'm not sure my gratitude was really heart-felt. That came later.

I've learned that there is a difference between being thankful and having gratitude. Thankfulness is directed toward something that happened or was given. It is targeted to a specific person, event, or object. Gratitude, on the other hand, is much deeper. It's a state of consciousness, a way of being, and doesn't require a specific event.

People who live in a state of gratitude have found a way to live in a state of perpetual contentment with life. They find ways to be grateful in each moment.

When we cultivate this attitude of gratitude, our minds and our hearts are in tune with this peaceful energy, no matter what circumstances are occurring at any given moment. Gratitude becomes the background music of our lives.

We develop an attitude of gratitude through practice. Here are some ways to get started. Each evening, write down five things that you are grateful for. Each morning, before getting out of bed, spend a few moments just thinking of all you are grateful for. Allow yourself to notice the small moments that enrich your day—don't take anything for granted.

The more you live in gratitude, the more reasons you will find to be grateful. And your life will be incredibly richer.

Worry a little bit each day
and in a lifetime you will
lose a couple of years.
If something is wrong,
fix it if you can. But train
yourself not to worry.
Worry never fixes anything.

MARY HEMINGWAY
1908–1986
Journalist, freelance writer for magazines, editor. Fourth wife of Ernest Hemingway.

Worry gets us nowhere. It focuses our energy on the worst possible outcome. When we worry we forget all about the possibilities, the opportunities, and the good that can come out of the situation. We live in fear.

One night, on an episode of *Everybody Loves Raymond*, Raymond had anguished for a long time over what to buy his dad for his birthday. He finally decided on what he thought was the perfect gift—a fish tank filled with beautiful fish.

His father loved it. Raymond was so happy!

Later that night, he and his wife were talking about the day. Rather than being grateful that he'd found the perfect gift, Raymond began to worry.

"Oh, no...now I have to top this next year. Dad will expect something even better! How am I going to be able to find something better than this?"

His wife, with an amused glint in her eye, turned to him and said, "Well, Raymond, you don't have to worry about it for another year."

Raymond looked shocked. "Oh, no...You clearly don't understand worrying—-this means I have a *whole year to worry about it!*"

Does this sound familiar? Do you get sucked into the vortex of worry? Do you catastrophize?

Letting go of worry puts our focus back where it belongs— on the magnificent possibilities and opportunities life offers us.

Begin doing what you want to do now. We are not living in eternity. We have only this moment, sparking like a star in our hand...and melting like a snowflake. Let us use it before it is too late.

MARIE BEYNON RAY
1891–1969
Editor, author, advertising businesswoman. Managing editor of *Vogue* (1911–1921) and associate editor of *Harper's Bazaar* (1921–1926). Author of *Doctors of the Mind: The Story of Psychiatry* (1942), *How Never to Be Tired, or Two Lifetimes in One* (1938), and other self-help books.

Living with Joy and Fulfillment

We all know how important it is to stay focused in the now. Yet how do we do this? How do we stay focused in the present moment? It's simple. Be where your body is! Just *be where your body is*. Most of us spend a large portion of our lives living in yesterday and tomorrow, and missing out on today.

My sweetie and I were going to the theater one night, and we were pulling into the parking lot. My mind was racing ahead. I said, "I wonder if we're in the orchestra or in the balcony. I hope we're in good seats." My sweetie turned to me and said, "Honey, we're in the car." This was a gentle reminder to be present in the moment.

You might be thinking "no real harm done, right?" But I missed out on the opportunity to be fully present with my sweetie in the car that night because my mind was wondering about who we'd run into in the lobby, where we'd be seated, and how the evening would be.

I have to wonder what other juicy life experiences I've missed out on because my mind was somewhere else, and I was "un-conscious." Only when we are right here, right now, are we totally experiencing our lives. There's a great amount of richness that we don't experience when we are not where our bodies are.

Will you experience the moments of your life or will you miss them? Commit right now to be present to the depth of the present moment and all it has to offer.

I love myself when I am laughing.

ZORA NEALE HURSTON
1891–1960

Writer, folklorist, and anthropologist. Part of the Harlem Renaissance. The most prolific African American woman writer of her time, her best-known novel is *Their Eyes Were Watching God*.

Living with Joy and Fulfillment

We all love to laugh. From giggles to guffaws, laughter allows us to express joy, release tension, and connect with other people.

Research shows the medical benefits of laughter. Laughter enhances our immune system, thereby increasing our ability to fight disease. It reduces levels of epinephrine (the stress hormone) in our bodies and lowers blood pressure.

Laughter even has fitness benefits! Hearty laughter exercises the lungs and increases the amount of oxygen in the blood. Researchers estimate that laughing 100 times is equal to 10 minutes on the rowing machine or 15 minutes on an exercise bike. Wow!

There are also amazing psychological benefits. According to the American Association for Therapeutic Humor, laughter gives people a way to release emotions such as anger, sadness, and fear, rather than keeping them bottled inside.

Laughter also provides connection. Life doesn't get much better than sharing laughter with a child or with someone we love.

How can you increase the laughter in your life?

Let your unrestrained enthusiasm pour forth in your laughter. Reap the medical and fitness benefits while you add joy to your life. Don't laugh politely—laugh with gusto!

There is a fountain of youth;
it is your mind, your talents,
the creativity you bring
to your life and the lives
of the people you love.
When you learn to tap
this source you will truly
have defeated age.

S O P H I A   L O R E N
1934–
Italian-born film star. Has acted in more than one hundred films over fifty years.
First performer ever to win a Best Actress Academy Award for a foreign film.
Received an Honorary Oscar for Lifetime Achievement in 1990.

W e can do what we love at any age. We can bring our joy, passion and excitement to everything we do throughout our lives.

I was reminded of this when I read about a gathering of 400 Hell's Angels in Gunnison, Colorado. It was described in the article as a cross between a corporate business meeting and a family reunion.

You see, this group of Hell's Angels had aged. It had been fifty-four years since the Hell's Angels had started, and many were now eligible for AARP cards! The article quipped that their "old ladies" really are.

Sunny Barger was the sixty-four-year-old figurehead of the group. He wore bifocals and had had a heart bypass. One aging sixty+ biker with a gray, receding hairline had traded to a smoother model, saying his previous bike had vibrated his dentures too much.

Harold, a tall lanky truck driver from Denver explained, "We want smooth and dependable—we don't want sore butts!"

These Hell's Angels had simply modified their equipment as they grew older, but were still engaging in their passion. I think they set a great example!

As we mature, we can find deeper ways to love and wiser ways to live. We can become more aware of what truly matters to us. We can share ourselves with generosity and strength. We can focus our energy and attention on the people and activities that are meaningful to us.

Let's commit to be in the prime of our lives at every age!

Forgiveness is all-powerful. Forgiveness heals all ills.

CATHERINE PONDER
1927–

Author of over a dozen books on abundance, beginning with *The Dynamic Laws of Prosperity*. A Unity minister who has served in Unity Churches since the mid 1950s, she heads a global ministry in Palm Desert, California.

You hear a lot about forgiveness in most spiritual teachings. There's good reason for that. Forgiveness opens the blockages that resentment and blame create.

It is not in your best interest to hold on to anger, resentment, and fear. They suck your energy. They burden your heart. They create illness and disease in your body. They steal the joy and beauty from your life and leave you mired in despair and sadness.

Forgiveness is not for the other person, it's for you. Let me repeat that. Forgiveness is not for the other person, it's for you!

The key to letting go of resentment and blame is to realize whose life is being impacted by carrying them around. Do you really want to continue to let that person or that situation have that much power in your life?

It is critical to our emotional and spiritual well-being to learn to forgive. At some point in our lives, we have to forgive our parents for the way they raised us—they did the best they could, given who they were, what they knew, and what they had modeled for them in their families.

What are you getting out of hanging on to the grievance and the need to punish "them," whoever "them" is? What would you gain if you let go and forgave them?

I think it's the Course in Miracles that asks, "Do you want to be right or do you want to be happy?" I'd rather be happy.

And that requires me to forgive.

Research tells us that fourteen out of any ten individuals like chocolate.

SANDRA BOYNTON
1953–

Greeting-card designer, selling as many as fifty to eighty million cards a year. Writer and illustrator of children's books. Song writer. Cartoonist. Author of *Chocolate: The Consuming Passion*, which she says was "largely motivated by the allure of having all my chocolate expenses be tax deductible for a year."

Women have a special relationship with chocolate—some call it a love affair. Chocolate's smooth, velvety texture sensuously melts on our tongue while its ambrosial aroma fills our senses. It brings us comfort, indulgence, and delight. We luxuriate in the seductive experience of slowly savoring a piece of good chocolate.

Chocolate is made from the seeds of the tropical tree, *Theobroma cacao*. The Greek term *theobroma* means "food of the gods." In Aztec society, cacoa beans were used to make a hot, frothy beverage reserved for warriors, priests, and nobility. It was a sacred concoction associated with wisdom and fertility.

Debra Waterhouse, a registered dietitian and author of the book *Why Women Need Chocolate,* believes it's a combination of cultural conditioning and chemical influences that impact our relationship with chocolate.

A comprehensive review of chocolate research published in 1999 by the American Dietetic Association came to the same conclusion. The researchers found that a combination of things influence our cravings—emotions, social values, sensory qualities, chemicals, and women's hormonal cycles. One survey even found that fifty percent of women would choose chocolate over sex!

So, next time you indulge in a perfect piece of chocolate—as you are captivated by its silky texture, as it ravishes your taste buds with its seductive flavor, as you give yourself to its hedonistic pleasures—know that you are in good company. You are joined with other women in abandoning yourself to the heavenly experience of chocolate.

The past is finished.
There is nothing to be
gained by going over it.
Whatever it gave us
in the experiences it
brought us was something
we had to know.

REBECCA BEARD
1885–?
Medical doctor and metaphysical healer. Widely known in the 1950s as a speaker and teacher of spiritual healing. Her writings, including *Everyman's Search* (1950), and *Everyman's Goal: The Expanded Consciousness* (1951), strongly influenced Norman Vincent Peale, author of *The Power of Positive Thinking*.

Most of us are not fully in the present. Our minds are in the future worrying about what hasn't happened yet, or in the past messing around with our history— reliving it or trying to change it. The truth is that only when we are right here, right now, can we fully experience our lives. If you are living in the past, you're missing your life!

How much time do you spend trying to change your past? I'll let you in on a profound secret I learned from Dr. Kennedy Shultz, a great metaphysical teacher: *"Yesterday ended last night."*

The only place that your past exists is in your own mind. Let it go. Bring those lessons into today, learn what you can—then leave the past where it belongs. Don't waste your precious life moments trying in vain to change what's already happened. There's nothing you can do today to change the past.

All of your life experiences have brought you to where you are right now. All of them. No matter what those experiences were, what matters now is "What did I learn?" and "How can I use this experience for my good?"

So look back over your life experiences. Let even the difficult ones serve you as you move forward. And remember, *yesterday ended last night.*

Nature has been for me, for as long as I can remember, a source of solace, inspiration, adventure, and delight; a home, a teacher, a companion.

LORRAINE ANDERSON
1952–

Writer, and editor of several books of women's writings on nature, including *At Home on This Earth: Two Centuries of U.S. Women's Nature Writing* and *Sisters of the Earth: Women's Prose and Poetry about Nature.*

My friend Brad and I had the opportunity to hike along the Columbia River which divides Oregon and Washington. It's breathtaking there! Our hearts filled with joy at the lush green forests, the gorgeous river, and the incredibly powerful waterfalls.

We climbed to the top of the highest waterfall in the country, Multnomah Falls. Along the way, surrounded by indescribable beauty, we began to pay attention to the lessons nature was teaching us.

Around every corner, there's a new vista. The trail to the top of this waterfall had many curves and turns. At each curve, we'd see an even more beautiful vista. We learned not to hold on to any one view, because there are new, even more beautiful ones to discover. *We can always be open to a new idea, a new experience, a new way of being.*

Don't impose how it "ought to be" on the way it is. We learned to open our hearts and souls to the present moment, and to release our expectations of how it "should be." Each step of our hike brought its own wonder, its own magic, its own delight. All we had to do was to remain open and present. *We can live our lives in the present moment, delighting in the "juicy-ness" of each experience.*

Allow others to be where they are. I was a slower hiker than Brad, and apologized to him when I needed to rest. He simply said "it's not a race," and we'd rest, and then continue our journey upward. We learned that the beauty of our surroundings and the joy of our friendship were what was important, not any expectations we might have of each other. *We can release the people in our lives to simply be themselves.*

My heart is filled with gratitude for the lessons nature shares with us each day. May our hearts stay open to these gifts.

Joy is what happens
to us when we allow
ourselves to recognize how
good things really are.

MARIANNE WILLIAMSON
1952–

Internationally acclaimed author and lecturer. Four of her eight books have been
#1 New York Times bestsellers. Founded Project Angel Food and co-founded the
Global Renaissance Alliance, a worldwide network of peace activists.

  **Living with Joy and Fulfillment**

When we pay attention to all of the things that are going right in our lives, we are filled with a sense of joy. Gratitude is not just something to do on the third Thursday in November—it's a way of being that enables us to live our lives with a sense of wonder, and to tune in to how good things really are.

We can practice "unconditional gratitude." This is gratitude that doesn't depend on any given set of circumstances. The Bible tells us "in all things give thanks." Not *for* all things—*in* all things. The great metaphysical teacher Kennedy Shultz said, "Rather than being carried mindlessly away by the good things, or driven into the ground by the bad things, take the time in the midst of all things to be grateful to God that you are greater than both the best of them and the worst of them, and that you will find a way to come out of any of them, somehow enhanced by the experience."

So we don't have to clog up our minds with the fear that the good things won't last forever, or that the bad things will. We just take time in the midst of all things to be grateful that there is a divine wisdom at work within us that knows how to use all of our experiences for our highest good.

I remember many times when I've felt resentful or down in the dumps and have chosen to count my blessings and get in touch with all that I am grateful for in my life. Almost immediately, I feel better. As soon as I feel gratitude, everything changes. I feel energized, my heart feels full and I tune in to the energy of joy. The very same situation can be transformed when viewed with a heart filled with gratitude.

Gratitude is always a choice. When we express gratitude, we draw to us people and situations to be grateful for. This is the magic of gratitude—so, *in* all things, give thanks— and revel in the joy of life.

Life isn't a matter of milestones, but of moments.

ROSE KENNEDY
1890–1995

Matriarch of the Kennedy family. Mother of nine children, including Senator Edward Kennedy, Robert F. Kennedy, and John F. Kennedy, our thirty-fifth president..

How many times have you said something like, "My life will be great when _____" *(fill in the blank).*

Do any of these sound familiar? When...

I graduate...my kids start school... I lose twenty pounds... I get married... I get a new job... I get a divorce... I meet my soul mate... the kids go away to college... I can buy a house... I make more money... I'm twenty-one... I can retire... I can take a vacation... my work begins to sell... we move out of this neighborhood... I find a spiritual community... I have more friends.

We wait for those milestones, and we miss the moments. In today's fast-paced world, we often feel pressure to multitask and accomplish more. We can talk on the phone, answer email, write a report, eat our lunch and straighten up our desk at the same time. But what do we miss?

If we begin to live the moments of our lives with care and attention, life gives us the true nourishment we crave. There is a great amount of joy and richness that goes unnoticed when we hurry.

Early one morning I was driving to facilitate a workshop for IBM in Boulder. As I headed west, the sunrise behind me was reflected on the majestic mountains in front of me. My eyes welled with tears as I took in the indescribable beauty. I pulled over to savor the moment and to bask in the early morning light. I still remember that moment three years later.

Start today to savor the moments of your life. Let them bring your soul joy and nourishment. Be fully present in each encounter with another human being. Promise yourself you'll stop waiting for the milestones.

I am beginning to learn that it is the sweet, simple things of life which are the real ones after all.

LAURA INGALLS WILDER
1867–1957
Author of books for children. Best known for her chronological series of nine novels loosely based on her life growing up and living on the American prairie in the late 1800s—the "Little House" books.

The wildfire had been burning out of control for days, and was nowhere near contained. We watched in horror as the news footage showed devastating images of blackened forests, and homes that had been destroyed by the flames. I wondered about the wildlife, hoping the animals had escaped.

Depending on which way the wind blew the fire, there was a possibility we might have to evacuate in the next twenty-four hours.

"What do you think we should take?" I asked, knowing we'd have to narrow it down to what could fit in our two cars. We began to have a serious conversation about what mattered most.

Our pets, of course, and some family mementos. The photographs of our families, our friends, and our life together. Our computers, because we both run businesses from our home. A few important papers. And as much of the artwork we'd collected in our travels as we could fit in and on top of the cars.

As we looked around our home, we realized that aside from these few things, there was nothing that was irre-placeable. What really mattered were the people and animals in our lives, and those things that connected us to them and to our past.

The rest was just "stuff." Sure, it was stuff that allowed us to live in comfort and enjoy our home, but it really was just stuff. Fortunately, the fire was contained before it got to Fort Collins. But that lesson remains with me—focus on what matters most, the rest is just "stuff."

Look around your home and your life. What matters most to you?

Living with Joy and Fulfillment

Some people go through life trying to find out what the world holds for them only to find out too late that it's what they bring to the world that really counts.

L.M. MONTGOMERY
author of children's books

Life is just a short walk from the cradle to the grave—and it sure behooves us to be kind to one another along the way.

ALICE CHILDRESS
playwright, novelist, actress, director, children's book author

It is those who have a deep and real inner life who are best able to deal with the irritating details of outer life.

EVELYN UNDERHILL
British writer

One can get just as much exultation in losing oneself in a little thing as in a big thing. It is nice to think how one can be recklessly lost in a daisy.

ANNE MORROW LINDBERGH
writer, aviation pioneer

Normal day, let me be aware of the treasure you are. Let me learn from you, love you, bless you before you depart. Let me not pass you while I may, for it may not always be so.

MARY JEAN IRION
author, poet

There are very few human beings who receive the truth, complete and staggering, by instant illumination. Most of them acquire it fragment by fragment, on a small scale, by successive developments, cellularly, like a laborious mosaic.

ANAÏS NIN
novelist, diarist

Being True to Yourself

Do not follow where
the path may lead.
Go instead where
there is no path,
and leave a trail.

MURIEL STRODE
Early 1900s author and poet. Wrote *At the Roots of Grasses* (1923), *A Soul's Faring*
(1921), *My Little Book of Prayer* (1905) and *My Little Book of Life* (1912).

Being True to Yourself

didn't get the whole concept of snowshoes: "So I put these things that look like tennis-racket heads on my feet, and that's supposed to keep me above the snow?" I asked. I was skeptical. I had visions of the snow, like a bed of quicksand, pulling me below the surface and suffocating me in its frigid depths.

Assuring me that I'd be fine, my friends led me to a trail-head above Poudre Canyon. The views as we walked were mind-blowing—sparkling white snow, magical pines standing like sentries guarding the edges of the trail, humongous mountains dwarfing everything around them.

For the first couple of hours, we could see that cross-country skiers and other snowshoe-ers had gone before us on the trail. It gave me a vague sense of comfort knowing that others had presumably been here and survived. This snowshoe thing was growing on me.

Further down the trail we came to pristine, virgin snow. No one else had come this far. I was filled with exhilaration and awe as we continued our trek. I felt one with nature, and tentatively tried on this new feeling of invincibility. I felt like an audacious, gutsy, courageous woman as we broke new ground.

I reflect on this adventure often. It taught me that taking a risk and breaking new ground is infinitely more satisfying than playing it safe. It taught me to move beyond what's comfortable and experiment with new ways of doing things. It taught me that limiting myself to what I've already done hinders my growth.

I invite you to look for opportunities to blaze your own trail. It's a phenomenal feeling.

I'm not offended by all the dumb blonde jokes because I know I'm not dumb ... and I'm also not blonde.

DOLLY PARTON
1946–

Country music star and actress. Began her career at age twelve, and performed at Grand Ole Opry at age thirteen. Heads $100 million media empire. Dollywood, her theme park in Tennessee, celebrates her roots in the Smokey Mountains.

People can and will think anything they want about you. It has nothing to do with you. What's really important is what *you* think about you!

How much time do you spend worrying about what other people think? Do you let stereotypes like "women are the weaker sex" or "blondes are dumb" impact your choices? Do you mold your behavior based on your interpretation of what other people are thinking about you? Living that way is exhausting, and is a no-win game.

It's important to remember the truth about you:

At the core of your being, you are everything that is good and pure and loving.

You have a unique talent and point of view to bring to the world.

You have unlimited potential and are here in this life to be fully who you are.

Generally, if people are judging you, they are judging themselves even more harshly. They are unhappy with themselves, and look out at the world with judgment and comparison.

I once heard someone say "If you don't have a bench, a robe and a gavel, it's not your job to judge." What wise advice!

Other people can think whatever they want about you. It's really none of your business what they think. Know your truth. Let go of other people's opinions—it's your opinion about yourself that matters.

We need to find the courage to say no to the things and people that are not serving us if we want to rediscover ourselves and live our lives with authenticity.

BARBARA DE ANGELIS

Contemporary

Author, popular television personality, and expert in the areas of personal growth and relationships. Author of thirteen bestselling books which have sold over six million copies and have been translated into twenty languages. Writes regularly for many national magazines.

Most women find it hard to say "no." We excel at people pleasing. We are expert at putting everyone else first. We think we have to be Superwomen.

We are terrified of being labeled "selfish" if we think of ourselves. We hold ourselves to a standard that no mere mortal could ever achieve. We spread ourselves so thin that our lives become whirlwinds, and we're always exhausted.

Several years ago at a women's leadership conference at a large computer company, I gave the participants a list of ninety-two Superwoman Stress Symptoms, and asked them to do a self assessment. I heard gasps, moans, and sighs as these women realized how many of these symptoms they had.

What about you? Are you experiencing any of these?

Perfectionism. Non-assertiveness. Feeling unsupported. Overcommitment. Loss of meaning. Digestive upsets. Indecisiveness. Poor concentration. Procrastination. Feeling overwhelmed. Negative self talk. Feeling trapped. Easily discouraged. "The blues." Lack of resilience. Spacing out. Resentment.

They could indicate that you have a bad case of "Superwoman Syndrome." The cure? *Stop and think before you say "yes."*

Don't let "yes" be a reflex response. When you are tempted to say "yes," take a deep breath and take a three second pause.

Ask yourself if the opportunity you are saying "yes" to supports a balanced and satisfying life. Ask yourself if it meets *your* needs. If not, say "no, thank you."

It will probably be difficult at first. But as you begin to say "no" and stop trying to meet everyone else's expectations, you'll find a renewed sense of confidence and a new level of satisfaction with your life.

In a society that judges self-worth on productivity, it's no wonder we fall prey to the misconception that the more we do, the more we're worth.

E L L E N S U E S T E R N
1954–
Author, speaker, workshop leader, relationship and parenting expert. Author of seventeen books including *The Indispensable Woman, Running on Empty,* and *Expecting Change: The Emotional Journey through Pregnancy.*

L et's get together for lunch and catch up," my colleague Jessica suggested. Our lunchtime "catch up and brainstorm" sessions are always filled with laughter and great ideas so I eagerly whipped out my PDA and began to look for an available date.

"How about May third?" I asked. "May third! That's five weeks away!" "I know," I said, "I've got a lot going on."

We set the date and I hung up the phone.

I looked at my calendar jammed with workshops, out of town speaking engagements, program design, client meetings, appointments, writing commitments, web projects, deadlines, and conference calls. I began to question my sanity.

I recalled hearing once that we are human *be-ings*, not human *do-ings*. You couldn't prove that by me. I sure wasn't leaving much time for *be-ing*.

I began to ask myself some tough questions. I wondered if I was confusing my professional roles (speaker, author, consultant, spiritual counselor) with my identity. I evaluated how much time I spent actually *being* rather than producing. I examined the relationship between who I am and what I do.

I made some decisions. I committed to reclaiming my place as a human *being*. I resolved to place *being* as high on the priority list as *doing*. It takes constant vigilance, but I'm getting better at it.

Are you stuck on the hamster wheel of life? Are you trying to cram one last accomplishment into your day? If you are, it's time to take a deep breath and to reclaim your place as a human *being*.

We are the same people
as we were at three, six,
ten or twenty years old.
More noticeably so,
perhaps at six or seven,
because we were not
pretending so much then.

AGATHA CHRISTIE
1890–1976
English writer known for her detective stories with clever plots. In 1971, was made
a Dame of the British Empire. At the time of her death, she was the bestselling
English novelist of all time.

Who were you when you were a child? What was your essence? What was your inner truth?

As small children, we express ourselves fully. We laugh when we're happy, we cry when we're sad or hurt, and we tell people what we think and what we want. We eat when we're hungry, we sleep when we're tired, and we play like there's no tomorrow. We are exuberant. We live in the moment and are filled with wonder.

We haven't yet learned to censor ourselves, to edit ourselves, or to fit into anyone else's notion of who we ought to be. We haven't learned to pretend to be someone we're not in order to "fit in."

Then, slowly, the world begins to tell us who we are and who we should be. Over time, we internalize those messages. We begin to fit ourselves to what the world expects us to be. Little by little, we allow bits of our true selves to die. We lose our individuality and become sanitized versions of who we are.

Think back to your "pre-pretending" self. Embrace your true essence—the truth of who you are. Give the world the gift of the true you.

Dance like there's no one watching, sing like there's no one listening, and love like you'll never be hurt again. I'm not sure who originally said this, but it's a great way to live!

It's the soul's duty to be loyal to its own desires.

REBECCA WEST
1892–1983

Rebecca West was the pseudonym for Cicely Fairfield. A British-Irish feminist, she was a journalist, critic, and novelist. Known for her writings on the Nazi war crimes trials in Nuremberg, she was made Dame of the British Empire in 1959.

Being True to Yourself

In order to know your soul's desires, you have to listen. Your soul will speak to you. It will whisper to you in the still hours of the night. It will show up as strong intuition, as a "gut feel." It will let you know what its deep desires are.

Your job is to trust it. Your job is to listen to the voice of your soul and follow its urgings.

In the coaching I've done, I've often had clients come to me with a feeling of heaviness, a feeling that all is not quite right in their lives.

I wonder what they'd rather be doing. I ask them what their heart tells them to do.

And no matter what the topic—work, abundance, relationships—it's always the same. When they start talking about their soul's desires, they transform. They become excited as they describe the life they'd like to lead. They lean forward and become animated. Their faces light up and their eyes shine. Their entire being becomes energized. It's clear they need to embrace this passion and move in the direction of their soul's longing.

What about you? Are you willing to listen to the messages from your heart? Will you tune in to your soul's desire? What is your passion? Are you willing to express it? Are you willing to go for it?

Allow your soul's desires to enliven you and spark action. It *is* possible to live your dreams.

It is very hard to say the exact truth, even about your own immediate feelings — much harder than to say something fine about them which is not the exact truth.

GEORGE ELIOT
1819–1880

George Eliot was the pseudonym of Mary Ann Evans Cross. British novelist, translator, and religious writer. Regarded as one of the leading thinkers of her day. Reflecting her background, she wrote about English country people and small towns. Known for her rich characterization.

D o you play "guess what's on my mind?" Do the people in your life have to try to figure out what you are thinking or feeling because you're not telling them your truth?

To live powerfully, we have to be willing to communicate clearly and directly. We have to quit beating around the bush and hinting at what we really mean. We have to let people know what we think and how we feel.

As women, we are socialized to "be nice," to "get along," and not to hurt anyone else's feelings. Many of us spend large amounts of time gauging the other person's probable reactions and responses before we even say anything. We dilute our message so there is not even a remote possibility that we'd be seen as disagreeable.

We censor ourselves, bite our tongues, and withhold the truth.

Then, as we climb into bed at the end of the day, we wonder why we feel misunderstood, unappreciated and discouraged.

We use language that diminishes the power of our message. Have you found yourself using phrases like "kinda" or "sorta" or "I'm not sure but...?"

In a meeting, have you offered your input beginning with a phrase like "I haven't thought this all the way through but..." or "This might sound stupid but..."? If you find these phrases in your language, you are not communicating as powerfully as you could be.

Living powerfully means communicating clearly, telling the truth, sharing your feelings, and being authentic. It means you never have to play "guess what's on my mind" again.

The great thing to learn about life is, first, not to do what you don't want to do, and second, to do what you want to do.

MARGARET ANDERSON
1886–1973

After a career writing book reviews, founded and edited her own monthly magazine, which published avant-garde writers from 1914–1929. Later in her life, published three volumes of her autobiography.

was in Chicago recently, and took a taxi back to the airport. I started chatting with the driver, a small man with dark hair and a huge mustache, who looked to be about sixty years old.

I was curious about how he liked driving a cab. He told me that he hated it. He told me it was a miserable life. He ranted non-stop all the way from downtown to the airport telling me all of the things he despised about it.

I asked him how long he'd been doing it. His response? *"Thirty-seven miserable years!!"*

Thirty seven years! "I can understand not changing careers at this point, but why didn't you choose to do something different earlier in your life once you figured out you hated doing this?" He proceeded to tell me about all the circumstances that in his mind had made him stay at doing something he detested for his entire life.

There is no circumstance, no reason, no excuse for spending your life doing something that doesn't bring you joy and satisfaction. It's important to find your passion, to find what excites you, to find what fulfills you, and *go for it!*

We live in a limitless Universe in which all possibility is before us. Do work that you love...play with passion... love without limits...and live the life you were meant to live.

Let us remember that within us there is a palace of immense magnificence.

ST. TERESA OF AVILA
1515–1582

Sixteenth century Spanish Roman Catholic saint. Considered one of the greatest mystics and woman reformers of her time. Her writings remain classics of Christian mysticism. She was canonized in 1622. In 1970, Pope Paul VI named St. Teresa the first woman Doctor of the Church.

You have within you the essence of Divine Spirit. The Universe is expressing in you, as you, and through you in every moment. You don't have to learn or do anything more for this to be true. You are part of the divine fabric of life and love right now.

Deepak Chopra explains it this way in *The Path to Love:* "...every person is like a piece of gold. If you were a gold ring, a gold watch, a gold chain, you could say 'I am a ring, a watch, a chain,' but these are temporary shapes. In truth, you are just gold—that is your essence, no matter how the shape changes."

He goes on to explain that "...you are the Self, created from the same spirit that in infinite form is called God. You are one grain of gold, compared to which God is all the gold that exists, and yet you can rightfully say, 'I am gold'."

What you really are is an individualized expression of the Divine Essence. You are part of God. You are whole and complete just the way you are. There is nothing missing. You are simply Spirit in the form of you.

Your job is to turn inward, to discover and connect with your higher self, and to live from that divine center. You have only one purpose in life—to know and love the Spirit within you and to express yourself fully.

Celebrate and honor the song of your soul. It is the song of life itself—of love, wisdom, truth, and joy. Sing it with passion in your own unique voice, and share your divine essence with the world.

Dogs act exactly the way we would act if we had no shame.

CYNTHIA HEIMEL

1947–

Writer, humorist. Writes numerous articles and columns. Author of seven books including *Get Your Tongue Out of my Mouth, I'm Kissing You Goodbye*, and *Advanced Sex Tips for Girls: This Time It's Personal*.

When my life gets too complicated and I want to remember how to live simply, I've learned to follow Bud's lead. Bud is one of wisest mentors in my life. He lives totally in the moment, and is more true to himself than anyone I know. Bud's a beagle.

Bud is really clear about his life's purpose, even though he's never read a self-help book or been to a seminar. He knows he's here to love and to bring joy to others.

Bud is never judgmental even though he hasn't been to therapy and doesn't ascribe to any particular set of religious beliefs. Having a bad hair day? Bud could care less. Leave him home alone while we go out into the world? Bud is so overjoyed to see us when we return that he whimpers with delight, wags his tail as fast as he can, and treats us to lots of beagle kisses.

Bud has an uncanny ability to empathize, even though he hasn't been educated in emotional intelligence. When I'm sad, he comes over, puts his head on my knee, looks soulfully into my eyes, and sighs. When I'm excited, he exuberantly shares my enthusiasm.

Bud is an expert relax-er, even though he hasn't had any stress management training. There's nothing he likes better than to stretch out in a sunbeam, or to lie in the grass in the backyard and chill out.

Bud is a great communicator. He asks for what he wants, having no restrictive childhood messages to overcome. When he's hungry, he bangs his bowl. When he wants to go out, he stands by the back door. He's clear and unapologetic.

Bud's canine wisdom reminds me to love wholeheartedly and to be true to who I am. What a wonderful teacher he is!

Prayer opens our eyes that we may see ourselves and others as God sees us.

CLARA PALMER

Surgical nurse and anesthetist. Healed of spinal meningitis through prayer. Writer on principles and techniques of spiritual healing. Author of *You Can Be Healed*, published by the Unity School of Ministry (1937).

A distraught spiritual counseling client was describing, in minute detail, a challenge that she felt was one of the biggest of her life. I listened intently, then shared some spiritual principles with her and helped her re-frame some of her thinking. I then suggested that we pray about the situation.

Horrified, she looked at me and bellowed, *"Oh my God, has it come to that?!?"* I realized at that moment that to her, prayer was a last resort. It was what you did when you were in a wretched situation and were really desperate.

I think of prayer as the *first* resort. The word prayer comes from the ancient Sanskrit root *pal-al,* which means "judging oneself to be wondrously made." What a wonderful way to think of our one-ness with the loving spirit that is the essence of all life.

Prayer looks at the world through God's eyes. It centers us in the universal flow of life and reminds us of our divine nature. It places us in divine communication and touches our deepest heart.

Most of us were not brought up to pray in this way. We bargained with or begged a distant God and recited prayers by rote, often not even knowing their meaning.

Prayer has the power to transform our lives. It reminds us that we are greater than any circumstance we find ourselves in and that we are one with a power that is greater than we are. It enables us to see ourselves and other people through the eyes of Spirit.

Living a prayerful life has the power to bring harmony and peace into our lives. It allows divine love to flow through us out into the world. Now that's prayer as a first resort!

I could be whatever I wanted to be if I trusted that music, that song, that vibration of God that was inside me.

S H I R L E Y   M a c L A I N E
1934–

American actress who describes herself as "always in transition and always in search of truth." Began dancing at age two. As well known for her spiritual beliefs as for her acting roles.

Have you ever tuned into the vibration of the Universe within you? Have you listened to your own song? Are you expressing your unique song in the world?

Alan Cohen, in his book *Wisdom of the Heart*, tells a wonderful story of a tribe in Africa:

"When a woman in a certain African tribe knows she's pregnant, she goes out into the wilderness with a few friends. Together they pray and meditate until they hear the baby's unique song. As they attune to it, the women sing it aloud. Then they return to the tribe and teach it to everyone else.

When the child is born, the community gathers and sings the child's song to them. When the child enters school, the villagers gather and sing the song. When the child passes through the initiation to adulthood, the people again come together and sing. At the altar of marriage, the person hears their song. Finally, when it's time for the soul to pass from this world, the family and friends gather at the person's bed, just at they did at their birth, and they sing the person to the next life."

It is imperative that we trust our own unique inner being, our inner essence. It's important that we hear this song within us and give it expression.

When other people try to get us to sing their song, we must instead trust our own vibration, our own inner music. We can harmonize with them if we choose, yet we can stay true to our own spirit, our own song.

The more we are true to our authentic being, the more joyfully and easily we live.

I don't want to be a passenger in my own life.

DIANE ACKERMAN
1948–

Poet, essayist, and naturalist. Author of highly acclaimed works of nonfiction and poetry. Has won many prizes and awards, including a Guggenheim Fellowship, the John Burroughs Nature Award, and the Lavan Poetry Prize. Also has the unusual distinction of having had a molecule named after her—dianeackerone.

Being True to Yourself

A re you living a feisty life? Do you have a vision for your life that you are passionately moving toward? Are you moving daily into an even greater expression of the beauty of your soul? Are you experiencing joy?

Or are you just trying to get by? Struggling through life? Plodding along?

It's a choice! We can move from the passenger's seat to the driver's seat. We can choose in each moment what we will think and how we will live.

Here are some ideas that can enrich your life.

Have a vision. Having a vision for our lives allows us to live our dreams. It gives purpose to our lives, and helps us decide where to focus our attention, our time, and our energy.

Live in gratitude. A grateful heart brings us into harmony with all of life. Gratitude is a way of being, an attitude of mind and heart. Let gratitude fill your life with joy.

Be present for your life. Appreciate the gift that each moment contains. Notice the delight that is available when you stay focused on the present moment.

Give unconditionally from your heart. You can give freely, not expecting to get anything back, because your gift is that you gave freely. Give a gift to each person you encounter: a smile, a silent blessing, an expression of love.

Express fully. You owe it to your soul to express your deep truth. Be the truest expression of yourself that you can imagine. Be who you really are—fully and passionately.

Living True to Yourself

We would worry less about what others think of us if we realized how seldom they do.

ETHEL BARRETT
writer, children's book author

Our concern must be to live while we're alive... to release our inner selves from the spiritual death that comes with living behind a facade designed to conform to external definitions of who and what we are.

ELISABETH KÜBLER-ROSS
psychiatrist, death and dying expert

You must love and care for yourself, because that's when the best comes out.

TINA TURNER
entertainer

It isn't until you come to a spiritual understanding of who you are—not necessarily a religious feeling, but deep down, the spirit within—that you can begin to take control.

OPRAH WINFREY
TV personality, actress

Let the world know you as you are, not as you think you should be, because sooner or later, if you are posing, you will forget the pose, and then where are you?

FANNY BRICE
Zigfield Follies performer, comedian, radio performer

My recipe for life is not being afraid of myself, afraid of what I think or of my opinions.

EARTHA KITT
stage, song, and screen star

Your Thoughts Create your Life

Life's under no obligation to give us what we expect.

MARGARET MITCHELL
1900–1949

Won the Pulitzer Prize in 1937 for *Gone with the Wind*, the bestselling novel of all time. The book was made into a motion picture starring Vivien Leigh and Clark Gable.

Expectations can set us up for disappointment and resentment. When we create an idealized picture in our heads of exactly the way something should be, life rarely measures up and we're left feeling frustrated and dissatisfied.

One summer, my sweetie, my friend Nettie, and I were in Colorado Springs to visit the Garden of the Gods, an area of breathtaking red sandstone rock formations towering against the backdrop of Pikes Peak and intensely blue skies.

The picture in my head was that we'd get up early, grab a quick bite in the hotel lobby, and get there in time for me to take photographs in the early morning light— except I didn't exactly share my picture with my travel companions.

When we woke up, they wanted to go out to a leisurely vacation breakfast. It took us a while to get seated, and an eternity to get waited on. It was taking so long to get our food, I wondered if they were out back milling the flour for our toast.

By the time we got to Garden of the Gods, the early morning light was gone. I was irritable and grumpy, and I made sure everybody knew it. I stomped through the park not fully appreciating the heart-stirring beauty because I was stuck in a picture of how the morning was supposed to have been.

What was *really* important was that I was spending time in an awe-inspiring place with people I love. I wish I'd remembered that at the time. Instead, I let the picture in my head of how it "should" be ruin what it actually was.

As a result of that morning, I learned that holding rigidly to an idealized picture destroys my ability to appreciate what life actually offers me. My challenge is to not let inflexible expectations get in my way.

Never be afraid to sit awhile and think.

LORRAINE HANSBERRY
1930–1965

American playwright whose play *A Raisin in the Sun* (1959) was the first drama by a black woman to be produced on Broadway. It won the New York Drama Critics' Circle Award as the best play of the year. *Raisin,* the Tony-award winning Broadway hit, was adapted from her play. *To Be Young, Gifted, and Black* was produced off-Broadway from her writings in 1969.

Your Thoughts Create your Life

've come to believe in the power of the hammock. Women are under a lot of pressure. We are urged to live phenomenal lives, to "be all we can be," and to "have it all."

We are often juggling family, career, school, housework, volunteer commitments, hobbies, yard work, personal development, carpooling, exercise, meal preparation, and friends. We rush from one appointment and obligation to another, feeling overwhelmed and exhausted.

We don't stop to remember why we're doing all of this. We lose sight of what's truly important. We forget about the big picture, and frenetically make our way through our ever-growing to-do list.

I recommend the hammock. When my life is at its most crazy, when I've agreed to one too many deadlines or commitments, I go into the backyard and lie in the hammock. I watch the clouds float by and think about what I really want out of life. I think of what's really important. I consider where I want to focus my energy.

I daydream and woolgather, I ponder and consider, I envision and reflect, I fantasize and imagine—and I relax. And I come away from the hammock renewed, refreshed, and invigorated.

When I'm feeling so frazzled that I think I have no time for the hammock, that's when I need it most. I have to make myself take a break and go outside and just think.

How might your life be enhanced by time to simply think? Would you benefit from reflecting on your true priorities and what's really important? I highly recommend some hammock time.

I believe we are solely responsible for our choices, and we have to accept the consequences of every deed, word and thought throughout our lifetime.

ELISABETH KÜBLER-ROSS

1926–

Beginning with her groundbreaking 1969 book *On Death and Dying,* she is the leading authority on dying and grief. Her books have been translated into twenty-five languages, and she is the recipient of more than twenty honorary doctorate degrees.

People often don't like the word "responsibility." Yet it is really freeing to realize that we are one hundred percent responsible for our lives.

Let's look at the word "responsibility".

Response-*ability*

Responsibility is really the ability to respond.

Although we often can't choose our circumstances, we can choose our thoughts, our words, and the actions we will take. No matter what situation we find ourselves in, we always have a choice.

Understanding this frees us from victimhood! We can no longer stand by and let stuff happen to us, and then whine about our situation. We can choose how we will respond, and find a way to turn the predicament into something that will benefit us.

This benefit might be a new awareness of our own inner strength, a new opportunity to grow in ways we hadn't imagined, or a new resolve to speak our truth. It might be a chance to try something new, or to explore another direction.

This situation might prove to be the very thing that propels us to the next level of success or joy in our lives. We simply need to take *response-ability.*

If you can't change your fate, change your attitude.

AMY TAN

1952–

Born in Oakland, California. Her first book, *The Joy Luck Club,* won the National Book Award and the L.A. Times Book Award in 1989. Her work has been translated into twenty languages.

Your Thoughts Create your Life

It's been said that attitude is everything. Our mind-set—made up of our thoughts, our beliefs, and our perceptions—drives our behavior, and our behavior drives our results. So our mindset or attitude is critical.

Each of us looks at the world through our own set of lenses or filters. These filters are made up of messages from our parents, teachers, peers, religious institutions, life experiences, education, our culture, and the media. So we see the world not as it is, but as *we* are.

There's a wonderful story about two men who went fishing. One man was an experienced fisherman, the other wasn't. Each time the experienced fisherman caught a big fish, he put it in his ice chest to keep it fresh. When the inexperienced fisherman caught a big fish, he threw it back.

The experienced fisherman grew increasingly exasperated as he watched the man toss the big fish into the ocean. "Why do you keep throwing back all the big fish you catch?" he shouted. The inexperienced fisherman replied, "I only have a small frying pan."

Is it true that he could only keep fish that would fit in his pan? Of course not! He could have cut up the fish, used the other fisherman's pan, or gotten a new pan of his own.

He *perceived* that he could not keep any fish that was too big for his pan. He *perceived* that he could only keep small fish.

His attitude was—small pan, small fish, small fish-catching opportunities. His fate could have been changed by changing his perception and his attitude. Attitude *is* everything!

Fear is one thing.
To let fear grab you
and swing you around
by the tail is another.

KATHERINE PATERSON
1932–

Writer of children's fiction. Known for her strong characterization. Winner of the Newbery Medal in 1981 for *Jacob Have I Loved*. Received the National Book Award, and numerous other awards and honors.

My friend Chris is a minister in Kansas City. He is filled with creative energy and constantly takes on new challenges—sometimes really big ones. He has a wonderful life.

I wondered how he could approach all of these situations so fearlessly. One afternoon as we drove up the Oregon coast I asked him, "Chris, don't you ever get scared?" "Sure I do," he confided, "I just don't let my fear dictate what I'm going to do."

I couldn't breathe. My head felt like the roof of the car had caved in on it. I realized how much of my life I'd let fear run me. I thought of all the times I'd played it safe and not gone after what I really wanted because I was scared. My eyes filled with tears as I thought of all of the lost opportunities.

I made a promise to myself in that moment. I promised myself that I would allow myself to be afraid, but I would *not* let it stop me. I promised myself I would choose to see fear as a signal that I was moving out of my comfort zone to do something new. I promised myself that no matter how big my dream, I was going after it. I decided to live as if I wasn't afraid.

Shortly after that, I left my secure corporate job of ten years to run a nonprofit organization. The following year, I started my consulting and training company. And now I'm writing this book.

Did these things scare me? You bet. Did I let the fear stop me? Thanks to what I learned from Chris, I didn't.

What are you letting fear stop you from doing? Take one step toward what you really want. Don't let fear come between you and your dreams.

That's the way things become clear. All of a sudden. And then you realize how obvious they've been all along.

MADELEINE L'ENGLE

1918–

American author, best known for her children's books. Won the Newbery Medal in 1963 for *A Wrinkle in Time*. The movie made from the book was the winner of the 2003 Best Feature Film Award at the Toronto Children's Film Festival. Has also written novels, poetry, essays, plays, and an autobiography.

Last Fourth of July, we had a family gathering. There were about a dozen of us, ranging in age from two to seventy-three. It was one of those fun days filled with food, love, and on this day, some fireworks.

My bother-in-law had been shooting off bottle rockets and firecrackers with the kids. After a while, we took a break for lunch.

"No one touches any of the fireworks or sparklers until I am out there, do you understand?" Dave asked the kids. Each of them nodded solemnly that they did.

After lunch, several of us were sitting on lawn chairs in the driveway. Teegan, who was eleven, leaned toward me and said, "I sure wish I could shoot off one of those bottle rockets." "You know you have to wait for Dave," I said.

Teegan looked me in the eye and said, "I know...but I can still *want* to!"

I thought that was pretty darn profound. What Teegan taught me that day was that our desires are our own. They exist independent of anyone else. Just because we have no means of fulfilling that desire immediately doesn't diminish its power.

Our thoughts create our lives. If we focus on what we truly want and put our focus and attention on it, the Universe will provide the means for its fulfillment. Our desires serve us because they attract our good to us.

"Good point, Tee," I said. "You're right...*you can still want to*. Let's toss the frisbee while we wait for Dave."

What a lovely surprise to discover how un-lonely being alone can be.

ELLEN BURSTYN

1932–

American movie and television actress. Won Academy Award for Best Actress in 1974 for *Alice Doesn't Live Here Anymore.* Also nominated for *The Last Picture Show, The Exorcist, Same Time Next Year,* and *Resurrection.* First woman president of Actor's Equity from 1982–1985.

Your Thoughts Create your Life

I've had periods of deep loneliness in my life. After my husband and I split, I spent five years living alone for the first time.

I'd gone from my parents' home, to roommates in college, to a live-in relationship, to my marriage. I'd never lived by myself. Some days the loneliness crushed me. I remember the despair of realizing that no one was there to ask me about my day when I got home.

When the isolation threatened to overwhelm me, I started going to the movies on weekend afternoons. At first I felt like everyone was staring at me, wondering if I was "desperate and dateless." Over time, I began to enjoy these times with myself and cherished those afternoon matinees.

I learned to enjoy my own company. I stopped looking to other people to fill the emptiness inside me and began to do things I enjoyed—reading, watercolors, hiking. I spent time with friends, but also looked forward to the times I carved out of my week for myself.

I now know that when I'm spending time alone, I'm in good company. I enjoy this time to reflect, to chill out, and to get in touch with myself.

Are you using the company of other people to fill your inner emptiness? Or are you coming to them filled with life, ready to share yourself with them?

The best way to enhance your relationships is to start with the most important one...the one with yourself. How can you know yourself more deeply and enjoy your own company today?

There is no scarcity except in our souls.

SARA BAN BREATHNACH
1946–

Author of the #1 New York Times bestsellers *Simple Abundance: A Daybook of Comfort and Joy,* and *Something More: Excavating Your Authentic Self.* Named one of America's twenty most fascinating women of power and influence, by *George* magazine. Founder of the Simple Abundance Charitable Fund.

Your Thoughts Create your Life

We live in an abundant Universe. Our limitations are caused by the limitations in our own thinking. Just imagine yourself surrounded by limitless supply. And imagine that your thoughts and beliefs create a mental mold that is filled up by the Universe. What mental mold are you creating?

Is it a small mold filled with beliefs of lack and limitation? Do you believe life is hard, we are meant to struggle, and that you'll never have enough? Or is your mold filled with thoughts of one-ness with Spirit, of being a magnet for good things, and of gratitude for your blessings?

Kennedy Shultz, the great metaphysical teacher, defined prosperity as doing what you want to do, when you want to do it, with whom you want to do it, in the way you want to do it. It's necessary to develop a consciousness of self that says you are a person who is able to do this.

We need to create a way of living in which we know that whatever comes our way, we will use it for our good. Eric Butterworth, in *Spiritual Economics*, shares a lesson from the oyster. Sometimes grains of sand get inside an oyster's shell and start irritating it. The oyster will try to get rid of them, and when it discovers it can't, it settles down and uses its creative juices to produce a thing of great beauty and value—a pearl. No matter what the challenge or the loss, we can create value from it. We can get busy "pearling."

Abundance is not for some other people in some other place. It's for you and for me. According to Webster, "affluence" means "an abundant flow." We need to center ourselves in the Divine flow, and quit damming up that flow with the sticks and rocks of negative thinking.

Let's open our hearts and minds to the abundance of the Universe. Let's gratefully receive its gifts.

What a surprise to find you could shift the contents of your head like rearranging furniture in a room.

LISA ALTHER

1944–

Author of five novels which have appeared on bestseller lists worldwide, have been translated into fifteen languages, and have sold over six million copies. Also writes reviews and articles. Aims to portray the human reality behind cultural stereotypes. Reviewers have said that she possesses "comic genius."

Your Thoughts Create your Life

I woke up in my New York hotel room. Rosie, my favorite waitress, took my breakfast order. My workshop got rave reviews. As I was repacking my laptop after going through security at LaGuardia, the TSA officer asked if I needed help. I told him I didn't. He smiled, reached over, and zipped up the last inch I'd missed.

At the gate, a spiky-haired guy with a heavy New York accent asked, "I'm going to get something to eat—can I bring you something?"

As I sat in my aisle seat on the airplane, a small boy in a "76-ers" shirt stopped next to me as he boarded the plane with his dad. "Do you play basketball?" I asked. He nodded, and gave me a huge smile. I spent the day noticing the joy moments.

Here was my other option. As I prepared to leave my hotel that morning, I noticed the torrential rain. I began to worry, not knowing if my plane would take off on time later that day. After delivering my workshop, I rushed to LaGuardia. Going through security, I had to unpack my laptop, take off my shoes, and lift my heavy suitcase on to the conveyor belt.

As I looked at the departure board, I noticed that my flight was delayed thirty minutes. The passengers in the gate area were annoyed at the delay. They were cranky. As I sat in my aisle seat while the plane boarded, people kept bumping me as they went by with their carry-ons. This one little kid in a "76-ers shirt" dropped his basketball on my feet.

This is same day from two different perspectives. I chose the first version, and had a terrific day. Which way would you have seen it?

I have great belief in
the fact that whenever
there is chaos, it creates
wonderful thinking.
I consider chaos a gift.

SEPTIMA POINSETTE CLARK
1898–1987

American educator and civil rights activist. Often referred to as the "queen of
the civil rights movement." A strong advocate for empowering women. Dr. Martin
Luther King insisted she accompany him to Sweden when he received the Nobel
Peace Prize.

Chaos takes us out of our comfort zone. When we're in our comfort zone, we feel relaxed, confident, and at ease. But once we step outside of that comfort zone we can feel scared, vulnerable, and unsure.

I don't know about you, but I don't learn much when I'm in my comfort zone... I don't have to! It's as if I've pressed the cruise control button and am just coasting along. Yet when I step outside of that comfort zone I have experiences that provide me with the opportunity to learn something new and to become something greater. I've learned to lean into the chaos of uncertainty, as tough as it seems at the time.

A friend once told me about the transformation that a caterpillar experiences. She said that in the process of becoming a butterfly, the caterpillar undergoes cellular disintegration. Cellular disintegration—talk about the world as you know it turning into chaos! Yet without this cellular disintegration, the caterpillar would remain a caterpillar.

Moving from knowing to not knowing and allowing ourselves to experience a time of chaos takes courage. Ultimately, it is the very thing that can take us to the next level in our lives.

Next time you're mired in uncertainty and confusion, and your life feels like it's in disarray, ask yourself gently, "What transformation can happen here?" Allow the discomfort of chaos to be a catalyst for transformation and new opportunity.

Envy is one of the scorpions of the mind, often having little to do with the objective, external world.

BONNIE FRIEDMAN
1958–
Widely known for her book *Writing Past Dark: Envy, Fear, Distraction, and Other Dilemmas in the Writer's Life*. Her work is anthologized in many textbooks and collections on writing.

eborah is talented, sweet, funny, kind and loving. She has a devoted husband and two great kids. Deborah's home envelopes you with its coziness and warmth. Her third grade class made her a "Best Teacher Ever" award, which she proudly displays on her desk.

She has the life she'd always wanted. So I was surprised as she sat on my sofa expounding on her inability to feel good about her life. "I just never seem to measure up. No matter what I do, I never think it's good enough. I feel like I should be more organized, get more done, be a better mom..."

Deborah suffers from *comparison-itis*. It's a disease that afflicts a huge number of women. Here are the major symptoms:

You compare yourself to others, and constantly feel that you are lacking and "less than."

You feel that everyone around you seems to be happier than you are.

You think that other people have it much more together than you do.

When you suffer from *comparison-itis*, you compare your "insides," your inner self, with other people's "outsides," the persona they put out there for the world to see. And that's a no-win game.

The cure? When you find that you're comparing yourself to someone else, remind yourself of the unique gifts and perspectives you bring to life. Take a moment to get in touch with all the ways in which you are awesome and magnificent and extraordinary. Let your heart fill with gratitude for the good in your life. And watch the symptoms of *comparison-itis* disappear.

I realize that if I wait until I am no longer afraid to act, write, speak, be, I'll be sending messages on a ouija board, complaints from the other side.

A U D R E   L O R D E
1934–1992
Poet, writer, activist, educator. *Seventeen* magazine published her first poem while she was still in high school. Worked to preserve and celebrate African American culture. Chronicled her battle with cancer in *The Cancer Journals*. Received many awards and honors for her writing.

When I'm an old woman rocking on my porch wrapped in an outrageous purple shawl, sipping tea while gazing at the clouds, I want to have no regrets.

I don't want to be sitting there wishing I'd had more courage and taken more risks in my life. I don't want to find myself whining about opportunities I missed, chances I didn't take, and a life I didn't fully live. I don't want to be asking myself, "*Why didn't you just go for it?*"

I want to be savoring the memories of my life, looking back and thinking, "*Wow...I really squeezed the juice out of life. I gave it all I had. I went after what I wanted. I stepped out, tried new things, lived boldly and loved deeply. I've had an amazing journey.*" I want to delight in the knowledge that despite my fears, I pursued my passions. I want to know I lived with courage.

Sandra Ford Walston, the author of *COURAGE: The Heart and Spirit of Every Woman,* shares the medieval French word for courage, *corage,* meaning heart and spirit. I want to look back on my life knowing I fully brought my heart and spirit to everything I did.

I want to remember the times I was scared to let go of the old way and embrace something new, but did it anyway. I want to feel the joy of knowing that I shared my gifts and my truth with the world. I want to know that I held nothing back.

What about you? What do you want to be reminiscing about as you rock on your porch in your outrageous shawl? And what will it take for that to happen?

A FEW MORE THOUGHTS ON

Living with a Positive Attitude

Happiness is not a station you arrive at,
but a manner of traveling.

MARGARET LEE RUNBECK
author

Kill the snake of doubt in your soul, crush the
worms of fear in your heart, and mountains will
move out of your way.

KATE SEREDY
children's book author

I've learned from experience that the greater
part of our happiness or misery depends on our
dispositions and not on our circumstances.

MARTHA WASHINGTON
first U.S. First Lady

Everyone has inside himself a piece of good news.
The good news is that you don't know how great
you can be! How much you can love! What you
can accomplish! And what your potential is!

ANNE FRANK
German-Jewish diarist during Holocaust

Thoughts have power; thoughts are energy.
And you can make your world or break it by
your own thinking.

SUSAN L. TAYLOR
editorial director, *Essence* magazine

Believe there is a great power silently working
all things for good, behave yourself and never
mind the rest.

BEATRIX POTTER
children's book author

It's All About Love

Love demands expression.
It will not stay still, stay
silent, be good, be modest,
be seen and not heard, no.
It will break out in tongues
of praise, the high note that
smashes the glass and spills
the liquid.

JEANETTE WINTERSON
1959–

Novelist born in Manchester, England. Published her first novel, *Oranges Are Not The Only Fruit,* at age twenty-four, and was named one of the Twenty Best of Young British Writers. She adapted it for BBC television in 1990. Her novels, short stories and essays have been published in twenty-eight countries. Has won numerous awards around the world for her fiction.

"Now that I have my degree and a job...I'm lookin' for love!"

She was standing in line behind me at the post office, talking to her friend. She had an irrepressible grin and bright red curly hair that looked like it had been shot out of a cannon.

I began thinking about how prevalent that thought is in our culture. We look for love as if it's some neatly contained thing that we can find or get. Then once we have it, we want to make sure we don't lose it.

Love is so much grander than that. I like to think of love as a verb— as something that we do, rather than as a noun—as something we possess.

Love has the power to open our hearts and teach us things about ourselves we never would have known without it. In *Les Miserables*, there is a profound line that says, "to love another person is to see the face of God." Love has the power to create a sacred bond between us and another human being.

Although loving another person can have its challenges, it also has the potential to bring extraordinary joy and ecstasy into our lives. When we allow our hearts to fully connect with another, we present ourselves with a great opportunity to *be* loving.

How can you let the essence of love flow more freely from your heart? Think of the people that you love. Are there opportunities to be more loving? Can you love more deeply? Are there opportunities to *do* love in more luscious ways?

Embrace those opportunities. Allow yourself to grow in love, and let love sweeten and enrich your life.

Self-love is the starting point for everything.

SUSAN L. TAYLOR
1946–

Editorial director for *Essence* magazine, where she also writes the monthly "In the Spirit" column. First African American woman to receive The Henry Johnson Fisher Award, the magazine industry's highest honor. Inducted into the American Society of Magazine Editors' Hall of Fame in 2002.

L oving yourself gives you a strong foundation on which to build a life you love. One important part of loving yourself is making the time to engage in self-care. Nourishing your mind, body, and spirit and treating yourself with kindness and compassion are essential to living well.

Self-nourishment is the first step toward a balanced, healthy life. Make a commitment to create "me" time each week. What would bring you pleasure? What would make you feel pampered? What would be a demonstration of self-love?

I know it's tough to imagine how you'll fit it in. Give yourself permission to start small. As you enjoy the sense of contentment it brings, you can expand the time you devote to yourself.

Perhaps it's a long bath. Surround yourself with scented candles and play beautiful music. Put some oils or bubbles in the water. Allow the warm water to envelop your body. Relax into the energy of self-love. Remind yourself that you deserve this time. Spend some time appreciating yourself for who you are.

Maybe it's a quiet walk, allowing yourself to enjoy the solitude and losing yourself in your thoughts. It might be spending some time in a hammock with a good book. Perhaps it's writing in a journal, capturing your experiences, thoughts, and deepest feelings. Maybe it's pampering yourself with flowers and allowing their beauty and scent to inspire you.

Whatever it is for you, take a step now to invite self-care into your life. Find ways to cherish yourself, to celebrate yourself, and to treat yourself well. Bask in the warmth and the comfort of loving yourself. And know that you deserve it!

So much has been said
and sung of beautiful young
girls, why doesn't somebody
wake up to the beauty of
old women?

HARRIET BEECHER STOWE
1811–1896
Best known as author *Uncle Tom's Cabin* in which she portrays the evils of slavery.
It has sold more than three million copies and has been translated into twenty-two
languages. When she met President Lincoln in 1862, legend claims that he welcomed
her with, "So you are the little lady who wrote the book that started this great war!"

It's All About Love

I love the lines and wrinkles on a woman's face," Harold said as he explained what he finds attractive in women. "They tell me so much about who she is and how she's lived her life. Those young girls—you can't tell much about them yet—their life hasn't been etched on their face."

Harold was in his late fifties, and was taking his first tentative steps toward dating after losing his wife to cancer. "I want to see the wrinkles around her eyes so I know they've crinkled up when she's smiled. I want to see laugh lines around her mouth—I want to know that she can see the humor in life."

I was surprised to hear my friend telling me this. I figured that given a choice, men his age would go after younger women. I figured guys would be attracted to their unlined faces and their gravity-resistant figures.

My conversation with Harold got me thinking about the beauty of women as we age. As we reach the later years of our lives, our wisdom has deepened with each decade. We've distilled the lessons that life has offered us. We live authentically. We've learned to focus on what really matters. We care less about what others think, and more about being true to ourselves.

We've shed some layers of protection and ego. We've grown in confidence. We live with a level of grace and self-acceptance that eluded many of us earlier in our lives.

And yes, we've developed some lines on our faces that reflect our journey.

In a culture that worships youth, it's up to us to delight in ourselves as we grow older. It's up to us to appreciate the ripening and the mellowing. It's up to us to remember that we will always have gifts to offer. And it's our privilege to celebrate ourselves at every age.

Women's liberation
now means being liberated
from stereotypes about
what women want.

MAUREEN DOWD
1952–
Pulitzer Prize-winning columnist known for her insight and her acerbic wit. Joined the *New York Times* in 1983, and became a columnist for the newspaper's editorial page in 1995.

It's All About Love

I was listening to my cousin's daughter describe the master's degree program she was about to begin. Her eyes were bright and her blonde hair reflected the sun as she excitedly told us about the genetic counseling program that accepts only four students a year.

I thought back to my mother's generation and how few choices were available to women back in the 1940s and '50s. When I was growing up, most of my friends' mothers were homemakers who managed the household and raised the children.

My generation had a few more choices. I remember Mr. Citron, my ninth grade guidance counselor explaining that most of the girls in my class were going into teaching or nursing. Since my grades in math and science weren't so hot, he thought teaching might be the best way for me to go. And sure enough, I spent my first four years out of college as a high school English teacher.

Today, women have a new set of possibilities. Want to have it all? Go for it. Want to stay home and raise children? The choice is yours. Want to stay single? That's okay. Want to work part time, start a business, volunteer? Have at it. Want to do nothing? It's an option. Life today is like the Burger King® slogan—you can "have it your way®."

We can decide what's important to us, what we want to do, and how we want to do it. This is tremendously freeing.

So let the experts analyze our demographics, define us as a "niche market" and think they know what women want. We know the truth. Each of us is an individual with unique desires and talents. Our life is a "user-defined field." And we like it that way.

To love is to
receive a glimpse
of heaven.

KAREN SUNDE
1942–
Playwright who has been produced Off-Broadway, in regional theatres, on a USA
tour, and in ten countries in seven languages

It's All About Love

The Beatles had it right when they sang, "all you need is love."

Our true nature is to express love. Think of children. They encounter other human beings with unbounded enthusiasm. They share themselves unabashedly. Their hearts are open and they love without fear.

As adults, our hearts long to love everyone—but often we want guarantees. We want to know we'll be loved back. We want assurances we won't get hurt. In life, there are no guarantees. And if we are coming from a place of fear or lack, no guarantee would be strong enough.

When we come from a place of love, guarantees aren't necessary. We simply express our true nature by loving, by being love, by choosing love. We can't help being loving—it's who we really are!

Every act of kindness, every act of love, every act of compassion brings more joy and light into our world. Bring love into your every action—love as deeply as you can.

Love is the ultimate reality. It is the ultimate truth. It is the path to heaven on earth. It truly *is* all there is, and all there will ever be. Love is the answer.

Resolve right now to move from fear to love. Choose to express love in every encounter. And watch your life transform!

Even I don't wake up looking like Cindy Crawford.

C I N D Y   C R A W F O R D
1966–
Supermodel and actress. Founder of a multimillion dollar empire.
Class valedictorian, who almost studied chemical engineering.

Our culture gives women and girls blatant and subtle messages about the standard of perfection we need to reach in order to be "okay." The images we see in the media are attainable by very few women. Yet they often create a feeling of discontent in the rest of us.

I love the article "Blowing Our Cover" that Oprah published in the March, 2001 issue of "O" magazine. It described what it took to transform her from the woman who arrived at the photo shoot to the woman we saw on the cover.

It told of a photographer and his technicians, a fashion editor, assistant fashion editor, editor at large, design director, photo director, hair stylist, makeup artist and stand-in. Fashion options included two racks of clothes, "28 pairs of shoes, 23 shawls, 14 bracelets, a dozen pairs of earrings, and too many necklaces to count." All of this for one perfect cover photo.

Oprah wanted to let real women know that she didn't just stroll in "as-is" and pose, so it's not likely we'd all look like that every day.

I don't know about you, but I don't have this level of support when I get myself ready in the morning. It's me, my body, my face, the mirror, and a little bit of Clinique.

We'd be well served by remembering that we all have our unique beauty. Our challenge is to feel it.

Today, focus on the beauty of your body. Give thanks for your good health. Provide your body with healthy nourishment and exercise. Appreciate its beauty, feel its power, and go boldly out into the world. Who needs a whole staff when you look and feel this good?!

People change and forget to tell each other.

LILLIAN HELLMAN
1905–1984

Playwright and memoirist. A leading voice in American theater. *The Little Foxes* (1939) is one of her best known plays. Had a lifelong relationship with mystery writer Dashiell Hammett. Active in political and social issues.

It's All About Love

Have you ever stayed in a relationship too long? Many of us clutch on to the people in our lives with every ounce of energy we can muster. We don't recognize when it's time to let go, and to let the other person move on for their good and ours.

We let fear take over and make up a woeful story about what our life will be like without this person. It doesn't matter if they're a spouse, significant other, teacher, or friend—we're sure we can't live without them.

The truth is that we are always growing and evolving. Because of this, there will be a flow of people in and out of our lives. As we change, we attract people who connect with who we've become. And sometimes we have to face moving on from people who want us to remain who we used to be.

Some people will be in our lives forever, some for a brief period, and some for a time in between. We can learn from each of them.

When a relationship is no longer serving us, when we are not reflecting the beauty of Spirit to each other, then it's time to let go. And only when we let go with grace and with love do we create an opening in our lives for the next person to flow in.

Clutching on to an empty relationship because of fear of being alone does not serve us. Staying in a relationship because of duty, obligation, or fear is not in our best interest.

So embrace who you're becoming. Celebrate the changes. Let go of relationships that no longer bring you joy. And open your heart to new people, new relationships, and new possibilities.

It seems to me that trying to live without friends is like milking a bear to get cream for your morning coffee. It is a whole lot of trouble, and then not worth much after you get it.

ZORA NEALE HURSTON
1891–1960

Writer, folklorist, and anthropologist. Part of the Harlem Renaissance. The most prolific African American woman writer of her time, her best known novel is *Their Eyes Were Watching God.*

It's All About Love

*W*hat were we thinking?!" we exclaimed as we howled with laughter. We were sitting on lawn chairs overlooking the lake behind Annette's home, reminiscing about our lives through the twenty-five years of our friendship. As we looked back over some of the choices we'd made and the things we'd done, we'd look at each other, burst out laughing, and shout, "*What were we thinking?!*"

I cherish that afternoon. It reminds me of how rich my life is because of the friends I share it with.

The first friendship I remember was Joel. He lived across the street. We made Lincoln Log houses and tossed baseball cards to see who could flip theirs closest to the wall. With Joel, I learned to share, to take turns, to tell the truth, to listen when your friend is talking to you, and not to hit. This proved to be a great foundation for my later friendships.

My friends teach me extraordinary things about life and about myself. They help me see the world through their eyes. They lead me to new experiences, and invite me to question and to learn.

With friends, it doesn't matter how we spend our time— hiking, having dinner, seeing a movie, playing Scrabble, or losing ourselves in conversation—we share a sense of ease and comfort when we're together. There's a feeling made up of some combination of belonging, support, love, history, trust, understanding and connection that binds our lives together in some magical way. Friendship is one of the greatest gifts life offers us

Celebrate your friendships—and let your friends know how much they mean to you.

Where there is woman, there is magic.

NTOZAKE SHANGE
1948–

Ntozake Shange means "she who comes with her own things" and "she who walks like a lion" in Xhosa, the Zulu language. Her award-winning *for colored girls who have considered suicide/when the rainbow is enuf* was produced on Broadway. In addition to her plays, she has written poetry, novels, and essays.

Have you ever walked into a room full of women and felt the magic? Have you noticed the kind of energy that exists only in a group of women?

Women connect with their hearts. I think that's a big part of it. We crave intimacy and share our feelings. Our lives are a web of connections and relationships.

There's an astonishing level of depth and sharing in a friendship between women. We find acceptance and support, encouragement and comfort, inspiration and love in our friendships with each other.

In our professional relationships, women are each other's supporters, mentors, and cheerleaders.

Recently, a Northern Colorado chapter of the E-Women Network was established. I went to the first meeting, eager to hear Debra Benton, author of *Executive Charisma*, speak. As I entered the room of over fifty women I was struck by the enthusiasm and the passion.

These women leaders and business owners were there to meet each other and to do business with each other. Each one was looking for opportunities to help and support the other women in the room. There was an appreciation of the power of women supporting other women. The energy in that room was extraordinary.

As women, we can find new ways to support and encourage each other. We can love and celebrate our uniqueness as women. We can share our magic with each other.

Love yourself first and everything else falls into line. You really have to love yourself to get anything done in this world.

LUCILLE BALL
1911–1989

Actress and comedian known simply as "Lucy." Former Zigfield Girl. Launched her Hollywood career as one of the Goldwyn Girls. First woman to own her own film studio. She was the biggest female television star of her time.

As a spiritual counselor, people come to me with a variety of issues—careers, relationships, finances, health, school. What I've been noticing lately is that underlying a lot of these things is a feeling that they don't deserve the best. They're holding themselves back, they're getting in their own way, they've forgotten the truth of who they really are.

The only gift that anyone has to give is themselves—so be in love with yourself, knowing that when you give of yourself you are giving a beautiful, divine treasure. Only when we truly love ourselves can we deeply love another.

How do we learn to love ourselves? Not by thinking about it, not by analyzing it, not by planning it...but by *doing it.*

Here are a couple of ideas to help you be more aware of your love for yourself:

Write yourself a love letter as if you were writing to a lover. Remind yourself of all of the things that are great and wonderful about you.

Envision yourself bathing in a pool of love. Feel love enveloping you, caressing you, soothing you. See love radiating out from your heart to the world. Feel your one-ness in love with all life. Feel the connection.

When you begin to have self-doubt—when that little voice in the back of your head starts saying negative things to you—simply turn to the truth. You are an individual expression of Spirit, and divine love flows through you in every moment.

Loving yourself is the foundation of a fulfilling life. Make a commitment to excel at it.

I'm just a person trapped inside a woman's body.

E L A Y N E B O O S L E R
1952–

Stand up comedian. In the seventies, Elayne Boosler was filling in at the music and comedy club where she waited tables. Andy Kaufman caught her act, and convinced her to do stand-up comedy.

It's All About Love

From the time we are small children, society gives girls and boys very different messages about who they are and what behavior is appropriate. Our culture tells women how we're supposed to be.

Research shows that boys are taught to be independent and competitive. They are encouraged to take action, to lead, and to win. Boys learn to be aggressive, to function in a hierarchy, to take orders, and to resolve conflict. They tend to play in groups and teams.

Girls, on the other hand, tend to play one on one and have a best friend. They play games that require cooperation and collaboration—dolls, house, nurse. There are no winners and losers in these games. They learn to listen, to take turns and to share. Girls are encouraged to be nice, to stay clean, and to focus on relationships, image, and beauty.

The media reinforces these gender stereotypes. Men are portrayed as leaders, women as nurturers. Men focus on strength and achievement, women focus on family and relationships. Men lead and are smart and powerful, women nurture and are emotional and loving.

Whew! Although this is changing slowly in our culture, many of these stereotypes remain.

Ultimately, we are people. We have choices about how we behave, how we relate, and how we live our lives. We can worry less about what we "should" do and what other people think, and can focus more on how we want to express ourselves and live our lives. We can be true to ourselves, move beyond stereotypes, and live powerfully.

The Eskimos had fifty-two names for snow because it was important to them; there ought to be as many for love.

MARGARET ATWOOD
1939–

Bestselling novelist, award-winning poet, critic, essayist, children's book writer, visual artist. Author of more than twenty-five volumes of poetry, fiction and nonfiction. Published in more then thirty languages. Has won numerous awards for her writing.

It's All About Love

I love my sweetie and am grateful for our relationship every day. I love to hike in the mountains, inhaling the aroma of the forest, feeling one with nature and with all life. I love purple—it's a rambunctious color filled with passion and strength.

I love my friends, and the joy and connection they share with me. I love to lie on the sofa with a good book. I love to travel to new places and experience other cultures. I love to go to Rocky Mountain National Park when the elk are bugling. I love the warm, comfortable home I live in. I love to sing with gusto, even though I don't have much talent and I really sound best in the shower.

I love my parents, who are no longer with me, and am grateful for their love and guidance. I love to go camping and sleep in a sleeping bag and cook over a fire and make s'mores. I love my beagle Bud, who knows how to live with joy and abandon. I love to wear fleece in the winter—it's comfy and cuddly and warm. I love conducting workshops and helping people transform their lives. I love to feel joyful and grateful and passionate and loving and powerful and vibrant. I love my connection with God.

I love my family. I love to sit by a river and daydream. I love to get massages. I love to watch children play and laugh and discover their world. I love to sit by a fire feeling safe and snuggly with someone I love. I love a good game of Scrabble. I love to take photographs, capturing a moment or a feeling or a scene on film. I love my colleagues. I love to collect folk art—especially when I travel. I love ice cream and pizza and chocolate, although my nutritionist wishes this list was broccoli and spinach and tofu.

This one word—love—does not begin to capture all of the ways in which we dance with life. Where's Noah Webster when we need him?

A FEW MORE THOUGHTS ON

Living with Love and Appreciation

Because you're not what I would have you be,
I blind myself to who, in truth, you are.

MADELEINE L'ENGLE
author

Oh, the comfort, the inexpressible comfort of
feeling safe with a person, having neither to weigh
thoughts nor measure words, but pouring them
all out, just as they are, chaff and grain together,
certain that a faithful hand will take and sift
them, keep what is worth keeping, and with a
breath of kindness, blow the rest away.

DINAH MARIA MULOCK CRAIK
Victorian writer and poet

We love because it's the only true adventure.

NIKKI GIOVANNI
poet, essayist, lecturer

Love doesn't just sit there, like a stone, it has to be made, like bread; remade all the time, made new.

URSULA K. LE GUIN
writer, novelist

You can give without loving, but you cannot love without giving.

AMY CARMICHAEL
writer, missionary

The truth is that there is only one terminal dignity—love. And the story of a love is not important—what is important is that one is capable of love. It is perhaps the only glimpse we are permitted of eternity.

HELEN HAYES
actress

Living Your Dreams

Find something you're passionate about and keep tremendously interested in it.

JULIA CHILD
1912–2004

Pioneer of television cooking shows, and cookbook author. Brought French cuisine to America with her book *Mastering the Art of French Cooking*. In 2001, donated her kitchen to the Smithsonian's National Museum of American History.

My friend Steve was volunteering in his son's kindergarten class on Martin Luther King Jr.'s birthday. The children were coloring pictures of Dr. King.

Most of the children were coloring in typical haphazard kindergarten style, and lost interest after a while. They wandered off to read books and play in the science area.

Except for Kimberly. Kimberly worked on her picture with great concentration. She poured all of the creativity in her little five-year-old body into her coloring. She made Dr. King's suit orange, his tie purple, and his shirt bright magenta.

Steve watched with amazement as her creation unfolded. He bent down to compliment her on her picture. Kimberly looked up at him with her brown eyes shining, and informed him, "I was born to color!" This little girl knew what she was passionate about.

When I was seven years old, I asked my dad to set up a card table and chairs in the garage so I could have a "school." By the next morning, I'd rounded up a few neighborhood kids, and was teaching them to write their names, tie their shoes, and make necklaces of macaroni and string.

Over forty years later, I'm still living that passion in my career as a speaker, consultant and author.

If you weren't "born to color," what *were* you born to do? What is your passion? Are you pursuing it? If you are, isn't it great!?! And if you aren't, what's the first step you could take to move in that direction?

Imagination is the highest kite one can fly.

LAUREN BACALL

1924–

An actress who made her first film, *To Have and Have Not,* with Humphrey Bogart at age nineteen after being discovered by director Howard Hawks on the cover of *Harpers* magazine. Known for her sultry looks, her husky voice, and her marriage to Bogart.

Living Your Dreams

What is the highest possibility you can conceive
of for yourself and your life?
What do you have to do to make that possibility
an actuality in your life?

I heard these two questions many years ago from a spiritual teacher. He asked "What is the highest possibility you can conceive of deep down inside—beyond your doubts, beyond your fears—and what do you have to do to actualize that? What do you have to change, what do you have to let go of, what to you have to *be* to live that possibility in your life?"

Wow...those were some deep questions. They began a process of deep introspection for me. They led me to move from a secure corporate job to my dream of becoming a speaker, writer, and workshop leader.

He went on to say that the seeds of greatness are in each one of us. Greatness is for anyone who is willing to be fully and completely who they were meant to be!

In order to live that highest possibility, we have to be willing to let go of some things. We have to be willing to let go of any internalized messages that say we're not enough, we can't measure up, and we'll never experience the life we crave. We have to be willing to let go of ideas of lack and limitation. We have to be willing to let go of a self-concept that says success and joy are for other people, not for us.

So what *is* the highest possibility you can conceive of for yourself and your life? And what are you willing to do right now to begin to bring that possibility into your life?

I can remember walking
as a child. It was not
customary to say
you were fatigued. It was
customary to complete the
goal of the expedition.

KATHARINE HEPBURN
1907–2003
A Hollywood legend. Challenged gender stereotypes and conventions. Garnered twelve Academy Award nominations over a forty-eight year period, and is the only woman to win four best actress Oscars.

Sometimes it's tough to keep the goal in mind when you're feeling weary or frustrated, or like it's just not worth it. At that point it's important to focus on why you wanted to achieve that goal to begin with, and on how you'll feel when the goal is accomplished.

This past fall, we were in the mountains near Vail for the weekend. I asked around for a great afternoon hike. Each person I talked to recommended the same place. So off I went to hike up the side of a mountain to a magnificent lake.

I packed my knapsack with water and snacks, and started up the mountain with excitement. I climbed over rocks and boulders, bounding upward, taking in the breathtaking scenery. I was in awe, and felt blessed to be there—until I was about half way up.

That's when I began to get tired. My enthusiasm weakened. By the time I was three quarters of the way up, I was having serious thoughts about turning back. I began rationalizing, "I've already had a great hike—it wouldn't be a big deal to go back down now."

Then I realized what a waste it would be if I came all this way and didn't see the majestic lake. I thought about how I'd feel later that night as I reflected back on giving up.

So I kept on, making sure I tuned in to the crunch of the rock beneath my feet, the scent of the pines, the reflection of the sun on the rock. I wanted to enjoy every step.

And then, as I turned a bend, I gasped. There it was—a magical mountain lake. The payoff of the lake was wonderful, but the payoff of sticking to my goal and seeing it through was even better!

If you have made mistakes, even serious ones, there is always another chance for you. What we call failure is not the falling down, but the staying down.

MARY PICKFORD
1892–1979
American actress, director, producer, writer, and philanthropist. Called "America's Sweetheart." Film's first international superstar.

t's impossible to get through life without making mistakes. We will have errors in judgment, we will make bad choices, we will perform less than perfectly sometimes. The challenge is not to dwell on our mistakes and let them consume us, or to label ourselves "a failure."

Thomas Alva Edison was a master of dealing with failure. He said, "I have not failed. I've just found 10,000 ways that won't work," prior to producing the first incandescent light bulb in 1879. His persistence and willingness to try another way resulted in over 1,000 patents, including the phonograph, the motion picture camera, and the mimeograph.

Often our failures give us messages about alternate paths to take. At one point in my life I owned a tanning salon. Buying that business was not a smart decision. I bought it because the person I was in a relationship with at the time really wanted us to buy it. I had no desire to own a tanning salon, but wanted to make him happy.

Not surprisingly, given the reasons I went into it, the salon was not very successful. I learned that pursuing a business that isn't in my passion area is not a good path for me. I learned to trust my gut when making life choices.

This failure provided me with new opportunity. I moved on, returned to work that brings me joy and excitement, and learned some valuable lessons about myself.

When things go differently than you hoped, regroup, learn what you can, and move forward. There's always another opportunity waiting for you.

If your efforts are sometimes greeted with indifference, don't lose heart. The sun puts on a wonderful show at daybreak, yet most of the people in the audience go on sleeping.

A D A   T E I X E I R A
No biographical information found. Quotation source: *The Women's Book of Positive Quotations*, compiled and arranged by Leslie Ann Gibson.

ook mom—watch me!" I shouted as I stood on the edge of the high diving board. "I'm gonna do it!" All summer I'd been jumping off the low board at the community pool. Today was going to be my first jump off the high board, and I wanted to make sure my mom witnessed this momentous event.

I waited until I was sure her eyes were fixed on me. I put my toes right on the edge of the board, gave my bathing cap a tug so it would stay on, and took a deep breath. I jumped on the end of the board a few times to get some height the way I'd seen the older boys do. Then I held my nose, took one last jump and sailed into the air. After what felt like an eternity, I felt myself hit the water and continue downward almost to the bottom of the pool.

I used my arms to propel myself back up to the surface, and doggie paddled over to the ladder to get out of the pool. In my excitement, I ran toward my mom's chair as fast as I could, even though running was strictly against the rules. "Mom, did ya see me?" I yelled.

"Sorry honey," she said, "someone walked in front of me just when you jumped. I missed it." I couldn't believe it—she'd missed my jump. I was crushed.

What I know now, looking back on this some forty years later, is that my jump was magnificent, even if no one saw it.

I try to remember this when I put something out into the world. If I'm excited about something I've done, I can't let the reactions of other people dictate how I feel about it. I have to trust my own heart, be my biggest fan, and know I gave it all I had.

And my second jump? My mom was at the edge of the pool watching, cheering, and clapping. It, too, was magnificent.

There are people who put their dreams in a little box and say, "Yes, I've got dreams, of course I've got dreams." Then they put the box away and bring it out once in a while to look in it, and yep, they're still there. These are great dreams, but they never even got out of the box. It takes an uncommon amount of guts to put your dreams on the line, to hold them up and say, "How good or how bad am I?" That's where courage comes in.

ERMA BOMBECK

1927–1996

Writer, syndicated columnist, humorist. Pointed out the humor and absurdity in everyday life. Book titles include: *Motherhood: The Second Oldest Profession, If Life is a Bowl of Cherries, What Am I Doing In the Pits?* and *Just Wait Till You Have Children of Your Own.*

Living Your Dreams

've always wanted to work with children," Marie confided, furtively looking around to make sure no one was listening. "I wanted to teach elementary school." Her eyes filled as she retreated into silence and lost herself in her thoughts.

I gently asked why she never had, knowing she'd been working as an administrative assistant since her grown son was in nursery school.

"I never felt like I was smart enough. No one in my family has ever gone to college. Every couple of years, I'd think about it—I even sent off for a catalog from the community college once—but then I'd get my feet back on the ground and realize I'd probably always be a secretary."

As we talked, an image of the jack-in-the-box I had as a child came to mind. When you turned the crank on the side of the metal box, it played "Pop Goes the Weasel." And when it got to the word *pop*, the box opened and a clown popped out. Then you had to stuff the clown back in, close the lid, and start all over again.

I thought of how much Marie's life was like that jack-in-the-box. Each time she'd think of going to school, of pursuing her passion, she'd stuff her dream back into the little box and close the lid on it. She was filled with regrets.

Don't let this happen to you. Believe in your dreams, fall in love with them, commit to them—and be willing to do what it takes to move toward the life you dream of. It's never too late to pursue your passion!

Just don't give up trying to do what you really want to do. Where there is love and inspiration, I don't think you can go wrong.

ELLA FITZGERALD
1917–1996
Most popular female jazz singer in the U.S. for more than half a century. Sold over forty million albums, and won thirteen Grammy awards. Gave her final concert in 1991 at Carnegie Hall.

To create a life you love, it's critical to do what you're passionate about. Here are some questions to consider:

What is the biggest vision you can have for your life?

What do you feel drawn to do?

What would feed your soul and bring you joy?

When you let go of concerns about finances, what other people think, and what you think is possible, what do you dream of?

Most women don't go after what they really dream of because they can't envision how to get there from where they are now.

You don't have to know the "how"—your job is to focus on the "what" and let the Universe bring the "how" to you.

When you are really clear about your dream and you bring passion and commitment to it, you'll be amazed at the things that begin to show up in your life. You'll have new ideas. You'll connect with new people. New opportunities will present themselves. Amazing "coincidences" will happen.

Your job is to pay attention and to act on these new ideas. Each time you take action, you'll be one step closer to realizing your dream. You'll begin to develop new confidence in yourself and to see yourself in new ways. Your ideas about yourself and what's possible for your life will expand. What seemed impossible just a short time ago will now seem possible.

Make a commitment right now to get clear about what you really want to do in your life. In your mind, see yourself doing it with passion, joy, and success. Act. You deserve to live the life of your dreams.

I didn't get here by dreaming about it or thinking about it—I got here by doing it.

ESTEÉ LAUDER
1909–2004

Entrepreneur who began mixing face creams in her kitchen, and built her business into an international cosmetics empire. In 1998, she was the only woman on *Time* magazine's listing of the twenty most influential geniuses of business of the century.

Living Your Dreams

Many women wait until they're "in the mood" to take action. They wait until they're "motivated." They wait until they "feel like it." And all of a sudden months or years have gone by, and they wonder why they're stuck in the same place.

You don't have to be "in the mood" to make progress. You simply focus and take action.

What stops us? Often, it's feeling overwhelmed. We look at what we want to accomplish and it seems so big, so far beyond where we are today that it just seems like too much to even get started. So we do nothing. And we stay stuck.

To move beyond this sense of overwhelm, we have to "chunk it down." Take the thing you are working toward, and break it down into manageable chunks. Then put those chunks in priority order.

Start with the one that's the highest priority. That's the one you'll focus on. The others will be there waiting for you when you finish the first one.

Break that top priority chunk into do-able steps. Then ask yourself, "What's today's part?" That's all you need to focus on today—today's part—not the next chunk, not the whole thing, but today's part.

Make a commitment to accomplish today's action whether you're "in the mood" or not. Follow through. Pay attention to how good you feel when you get it done. Savor that feeling of accomplishment. You'll build on that.

Tomorrow, ask yourself again, "What's today's part?" Take action. Make steady progress. And never be stuck again.

Winning the [Nobel] prize wasn't half as exciting as doing the work itself.

MARIA GOEPPERT MAYER
1906–1972

Physicist and professor born in Upper Silesia (then Germany, now Poland). Famous for the understanding of the structure of the atomic nucleus, the nuclear shell model. Won the Nobel Prize (shared with Hans Jensen) in 1963. Second woman to win a Nobel Prize, after Madame Curie sixty years earlier.

A re you working with soul? In my consulting work I continually see people who hate their jobs, who are doing something they don't really love, and whose souls are slowly dying one day at a time because they are not fully expressing their creativity.

I hope you're not one of them. You have a choice. You are here to express who you are and to share your gifts and talents with the world. Find something you love to do and do it with all your heart and soul.

Buddha said "Your work is to *discover* your work, and then with all your heart to give yourself to it."

My niece recently became a certified nurse's assistant. She works in a nursing home. Her duties aren't what most of us would consider glamorous or fun.

Yet as she described her job, it was clear she'd found her soul work. "The minute you meet and work with the residents, you fall in love with them as if they are your own grandparents. They tell you stories and teach you things about being yourself. That's where I get the passion to love and care for them. They make me smile. I get to help them every day."

Christy has found a way to connect with the deeper meaning of her work. She knows how she makes a difference. She truly works with soul.

Think about the times when you've been truly motivated and excited by your work. Find the common threads in those experiences. This will tell you what it takes for you to have work that enlivens you. Open yourself up to opportunities to do the work you were meant to do, and give yourself the gift of working with soul.

I can do anything.
I can be anything.
No one ever told me
I couldn't. No one ever
expressed this idea that
I was limited to any one
thing, and so I think in
terms of what's possible,
not impossible.

WHOOPI GOLDBERG
1955–

Born Caryn Johnson in New York City. Outspoken comedian and actress who came to prominence with her role in *The Color Purple*. Has won numerous awards including the Oscar, Tony, Golden Globe, and Grammy awards. Also known for her humanitarian efforts. Her friends began calling her Whoopi (like "whoopee cushion") due to her flatulence. She took the name Goldberg after the Jewish side of her family.

Let's dream a little. Forget about your current reality—just close your eyes, and imagine what life would be like if you were living your dreams. If you could be and do anything you wanted, what would your ideal day look like?

Where do you wake up? How do you feel as you awaken? How do you spend your daytime hours? Imagine this in vivid detail. What are you wearing? Are there other people around? How do you spend your evening? What are you thinking and feeling as you go to bed that night?

This ideal day gives you a glimpse of the life of your dreams. What's stopping you from living it?

Are you letting excuses get in your way? Do you tell yourself that you don't have enough money, education, courage, or luck? Do you think you're not the right gender, race, ethnicity, sexual orientation, or age? Do you rationalize your unwillingness to step out there and "go for it" by talking yourself into the idea that where you are now is really not so bad?

Here's a sobering equation:

NO RESULTS plus EXCUSES does not equal RESULTS

If you're living a life you love, celebrate it! And if you're not, let go of your excuses and go after what you really want.

Your dream is your soul speaking to you, telling you to move toward your highest aspiration. Move from *impossible* to *I'm possible*. Live the life you dream of.

The most effective way to do it, is to do it.

TONI CADE BAMBARA
1939–1955

Writer, teacher, civil rights activist, and filmmaker. Born in New York City. Her writing had a strong focus on African American women. Authored several collections of short stories, and two novels.

I'm one of those people who can postpone getting something done for an incredibly long period of time. I can research it to death, talk to other people about their experiences, and find a myriad of other things to do before I actually get started.

I have good intentions. I'm looking for the best way or the right way to do it. I want to learn before I leap.

But I've learned that the best way to get something done is to take action, get started and do it. Often, once I've started I wonder why I postponed beginning for so long.

This book was like that. I had the idea a year before I actually started writing. I talked about it to friends, tested it with other authors, researched the publishing business, and went to workshops. I thought and dreamed about my book. I envisioned feisty women all over the world being inspired by these great quotations.

Then I read Stephen King's *On Writing*, in which he says, "...the hours we spend talking about writing is time we don't spend actually *doing* it." Oooops.

I knew it was time to sit down and face the empty piece of paper. It was time to begin this book and make my intention a reality. It was time to take action.

Think of the things in your life you've been postponing. What have you been meaning to begin? Go ahead—take the first step. Once you get going, it gets easier.

Security is mostly a superstition. It does not exist in nature, nor do the children of men as a whole experience it. Avoiding danger is no safer in the long run than outright exposure. Life is either a daring adventure or nothing.

HELEN KELLER
1880–1968

At age one, experienced a serious illness that destroyed her sight and hearing. Also unable to speak, and was shut off from the world. Rose above her disabilities to graduate from college and become an advocate for people with disabilities.

Many of us try to get through life by "playing it safe." We are afraid of failing. We don't want to give up control. We want to feel comfortable. And by doing so, we lose the opportunity to explore, to discover, to grow, to become more. It takes guts to let go of security and try something new. It takes courage to go after something big. It takes moxie to step outside of your comfort zone and go for it.

A few years ago, I signed up to do the Avon Breast Cancer Walk. Until that moment, the furthest I'd ever walked in my life was about three miles. This was to be a three-day, sixty-mile fundraising walk. Oh, did I mention I was overweight and out of shape? To top it off, I had to raise at least $2500 to participate.

It was quite an adventure. I trained for five months. When it came to the big weekend, there was incredible heat. Every few miles, a pit stop with Gatorade®, water, and snacks. Medical support and IV hydration for those who struggled. Porta-potties® and big shower trucks. Tents for night time. Moleskin and band-aids® and duct tape for my feet so I could keep going.

Although there were times I was afraid I couldn't walk another step, times I was tempted to jump in the sweep van picking up the walkers who couldn't complete that day's miles, I walked every one of those sixty miles and raised over $4000.

It was one of the most incredible experiences of my life. It was a weekend of huge physical challenges, and emotional and profound moments. It was a daring adventure.

What opportunities can you say *yes* to in your life? Where can you let go of "playing it safe?" What daring adventures are *you* willing to have?

Living Your Dreams

There are only three colors, ten digits, and seven notes; it's what we do with them that's important.

RUTH ROSS
author, therapist

Reach high, for stars lie hidden in your soul.
Dream deep, for every dream precedes the goal.

PAMELA VAULL STARR
writer, artist

My private measure of success is daily. If this were to be the last day of my life would I be content with it? To live in a harmonious balance of commitments and pleasures is what I strive for.

JANE RULE
British Columbian writer

When I stand before God at the end of my life,
I would hope that I would not have a single bit
of talent left, and could say, "I used everything
you gave me."

ERMA BOMBECK
humorist, author

Go ahead and do it. It's much easier to apologize
after something's been done than to get permission
ahead of time.

GRACE MURRAY HOPPER
admiral, computer pioneer

You don't need endless time and perfect conditions.
Do it now. Do it today. Do it for twenty minutes
and watch your heart start beating.

BARBARA SHER
author, motivational speaker

ABOUT THE AUTHOR

Ava Diamond is an acclaimed speaker and consultant. She is committed to helping individuals fulfill their true potential, and to helping organizations leverage the talent of their people.

Thousands of people have benefited from her high-energy programs on personal excellence, success strategies for women, leading in today's world, building extraordinary teams, thriving through change, and winning with diversity.

She delivers keynote addresses, seminars, and workshops to corporations, associations, women's organizations, governments, and professional conferences.

Ava has shared her wisdom with such organizations as: IBM, Pepsico, the City of Atlanta, the Elton John AIDS Foundation, Boulder Community Hospital, E-Women Network, Hewlett-Packard, and AT&T. She is co-author of *Real World Management Strategies that Work.*

As a licensed spiritual counselor, she has worked with people one-on-one to help them live with more joy and satisfaction.

For additional information about Ava's books and programs, or to schedule her for a presentation, please contact:

Diamond Success Group
Phone: 970-224-3015   Toll Free: 877-FEISTY-1
Fax: 970-224-2874
Web Site: www.avadiamond.com

ABOUT THE ILLUSTRATOR

Ilan Shamir is the creator of *A Thousand Things Went Right Today®*. He delivers keynotes and workshops that build positive momentum. Visit www.YourTrueNature.com to learn about his interactive keynotes and fabulous products, or call 800-992-4769.

Be in Ava's next book!

We are collecting inspirational, true stories from feisty women to include in our next book. For details and submission guidelines, please visit www.feistywomen.com

Share the impact!

Let us know how *Great Quotes from Feisty Women* has contributed to your life. Send us an email at greatquotes@feistywomen.com.

NAMES INDEX

Give

GREAT QUOTES FROM

Feisty Women

to your feisty friends and colleagues!

YES! I want _____ copies of *Great Quotes from Feisty Women* at $13.95 each.

FAX ORDERS: 970-224-2874. Send this form
PHONE ORDERS: Call toll free: 877-FEISTY-1
WEB ORDERS: www.feistywomen.com
POSTAL ORDERS: Mail this form to
     Sage Creek Press
     P.O. Box 8181
     Fort Collins, CO 80526

SHIPPING:. $3.95 shipping and handling for one book, and $1.95 for each additional book to U.S. addresses

SALES TAX: Please add applicable sales tax for orders shipped to Colorado addresses.

My check or money order for $_____ is enclosed.
PLEASE CHARGE MY
     ☐ Visa   ☐ Mastercard

NAME ON CARD _____

CARD NUMBER _____

EXPIRATION DATE _____

NAME _____

ORGANIZATION _____

ADDRESS _____

CITY / STATE / ZIP _____

EMAIL ADDRESS _____

TELEPHONE NUMBER _____

May these
quotations
provide you
with endless
inspiration...

Live Feisty!